From the reviews of *All th*

'arrestingly honest'
Herald Sun

'It's hard to fathom how mund[...]
Melbourne suburb, a mouldy [...]
can make for a rollicking read but then most of us don't have the
storytelling skills of stand-up comedian Denise Scott.'
Eleanor Limprecht, *The Sun Herald*

'Creating wry black comedy out of the memory of seeing your
grandmother drop dead from a heart attack or the temporary
breakdown of your relationship with your long-time partner is no
mean feat but Scott is fearless without being cruel or gratuitous. But
All that Happened is more than a string of amusing anecdotes. The
narrative is driven by Scott's honest examination of the challenging yet
worthwhile struggle to be a parent, partner and self-supporting artist.'
The Age

'This book shows exactly what it takes to hold it all together
when you want to follow your career, maintain the love in your
marriage, raise two children and look after an ageing parent. It is
as heartwarming as it is laugh-out-loud funny.'
Catherine Nikas-Boulos, *The Daily Telegraph*

'Number 26 is a cheerful and cosy home, and everyone seems to
get along. But it's the dramatic past events that make Scott's book so
absorbing: the affairs, career disasters, psychotic pets and wild parties.
She is a natural storyteller – which isn't surprising, given her 20-odd
years as a stand-up comic.'
Michael Lallo, *The Age*

'a hugely entertaining read'
Townsville Eye

'This is a book that could sit proudly alongside other justly feted
autobiographies such as Albert Facey's *A Fortunate Life* and Sally
Morgan's *My Place*, neither of which has a story to rival the tale of
cousin Gavin's brown bri-nylon underpants. Slip into Number 26
and spend a few hours in Denise Scott's chaotic, lovely world.'
Teacher Magazine

All that
happened at
number 26

Denise Scott

hardie grant books
MELBOURNE · LONDON

First published in 2008
This edition published in 2014 by Hardie Grant Books

Hardie Grant Books (Australia)
Ground Floor, Building 1
658 Church Street
Richmond, Victoria 3121
www.hardiegrant.com.au

Hardie Grant Books (UK)
Dudley House, North Suite
34–35 Southampton Street
London WC2E 7HF
www.hardiegrant.co.uk

A Cataloguing-in-Publication entry is available from the catalogue
of the National Library of Australia at www.nla.gov.au
All that happened at number 26
ISBN 978 1 74270 804 1

Cover design by Josh Durham/Design by Committee
Typesetting by Kirby Jones
Printed in Australia by Griffin Press

The paper this book is printed on is certified against the Forest
Stewardship Council® Standards. Griffin Press holds FSC chain
of custody certification SGS-COC-005088. FSC promotes
environmentally responsible, socially beneficial and economically
viable management of the world's forests.

For

John, Jordie and Bonnie

with love, respect and the sincere hope they

don't sue.

CHAPTER 1

First sighting
of number 26

'll never forget the first time John and I saw number 26. We just knew it was going to be ours. It was so awful and ugly and repulsive in every way, not to mention being in a suburb I had sworn I'd rather die than live in, that we knew we had a great chance of getting it. To be honest, the first time we saw the house was about ten minutes before it was auctioned.

The pressure was on. John's dad had made the big announcement: 'Now that you two have a baby, you can't go on living in these … um … run-down cheap rental properties; you have to buy a house.'

We were visiting John's parents at the time, sitting around their beautiful Australian hardwood dining table, having just finished an entire slab of pork belly. Oh my God, the crackling. My chin was glistening with the fat and I felt a little self-conscious taking yet another handful but there isn't much in life that gives me greater joy than crispy pig fat so I was determined to make the most of this rare opportunity; it surely beat the steamed vegies and rice John and I were used to. Meanwhile John polished off the remains of the gourmet salad that had featured such a variety of lettuce leaves that, quite frankly, I was taken by surprise: I had no idea there was more to life than iceberg. John's dad had just returned from the downstairs cellar where he'd been sent by his wine-loving wife to select another bottle of vintage red, which he then decanted into a crystal glass bottle. Out of the side of his mouth John quietly explained, 'It's so it can breathe, Scotty.'

'Oh, I see,' I replied, half-expecting to hear myself speaking with a cockney accent like Eliza in *My Fair Lady* when she's being taught to sing 'The Rain in Spain Stays Mainly in the Plain.'

The wine was then poured into proper red wine glasses and we had to roll it around and sniff it and say stuff like, 'Mmm, this one's got a strong nose … a bit woody perhaps.'

'What do you think, Scotty?' John's mum looked at me, eager to hear my opinion. 'Mmm … well … mm … um … I think it smells … very … um, very … let's see … very nice.' Silence. Deafening silence.

'Gee, look at the sunset,' John piped up, coming to my rescue. We all turned our attention to the floor-to-ceiling windows. The clouds had cleared to reveal a rare and perfect view of Wilsons Promontory, looking for all the world as though it sat precariously balanced on the horizon.

I couldn't help but ponder the differences between John's family home and the one I'd grown up in. Ours was a small war-service weatherboard in Greensborough. Well, it was weatherboard until the day I arrived home to find it had magically become brick. I'd always assumed it must have been Mum who insisted on the brick cladding but, as she explained years later, 'A salesman knocked on the door one evening when your father was drunk, and before I knew anything about it he'd signed on the dotted line.'

'The point is you need a house, John. You're thirty years old now, and you've got a family.'

'I agree, Dad.'

I looked up at John, who had produced his ukulele and was trying to work out the next chord in the Bushwackers' version of the song, 'And the Band Played Waltzing Matilda'. I had moved to a lounge chair so that I could sit somewhere comfortable and breastfeed our six-month-old son for the eighty-seventh time that day. My face was pale, my hair a dull mousey bob, and I had dark rings under my eyes. I was having a mild asthma attack, sneaking a quick puff of Ventolin when no one was looking. I didn't want John's parents to know about my wheezing as this may have led them to ask what might be causing it; I was reluctant to tell them that it was probably brought on by the conversation about John and me buying a house. And also that, tragically, it seemed I was allergic to their brand new, extremely expensive, 100 per cent Australian wool lounge chairs.

In retrospect, I'm also pretty certain that the dress I was wearing could have easily induced my asthma attack. It was a fleecy-lined frock I'd bought at the op-shop where, post-children, I did all my clothes shopping. It was aqua in colour and shapeless until the hips, where it was gathered into a skirt that came to my knees. I bought it mainly because it had large silver buttons down the front, allowing me to easily provide milk on tap to my big, fat, healthy baby. The fact that I was wearing it with navy ribbed tights and my old brown walking boots − one of which was bound up with gaffer tape because it had come adrift at the sole − has since caused me to wonder whether I mightn't have been suffering just a touch of postnatal depression.

'Of course, interest rates are on the way up at the moment but there's no point waiting for a better time. Houses only ever go up in value. You may as well do it now, John.'

'Yeah, Dad, I think you're right.'

I had another squirt of Ventolin. I tried to eyeball John but he just kept looking down at his uke. I tried harder. I tried with all my might to will that man to look at my face and read it. Please, John, please, for Christ's sake, please, please read my desperate face. Oh my godfather; it was hopeless. John had now moved on to an emotional rendition of Redgum's 'He Was Only Nineteen'. If he'd looked up he would've realised by my expression that I was silently screaming at him: 'John, are you completely fucking insane? How can we buy a house? We haven't got a single cent in the bank!'

I come from a working-class background; my dad was a deliverer of small goods and my mum a nurses' aide in a geriatric home. They bought their war-service, soon-to-be faux brick number in 1953 and never moved until Dad went to the afterlife and Mum to a dementia unit. I grew up with the strong belief that you did not even *think* about buying a house unless you had a job, money in the bank, or at the very least had risked your life in a world war and got a loan with really cheap repayments.

We had no savings whatsoever and John had been just a bit young to fight in Vietnam – not that those poor bastards got special home loan deals; they didn't even get a welcome home parade. But John did have a job. He was working with a street theatre group that required him to regularly dress up in full drag as a policewoman, play a trumpet and juggle three apples which, at the show's climax, he would chop with a meat-cleaver mid-air. Sure, it was a great act and he loved the work but the hours were long and the pay was crap – close to, if not less than, the dole.

As for me, I had stopped performing while I was pregnant. Soon after the birth, though, I did make an attempt to get back on the horse but my God, was it painful – and not because I'd had an episiotomy. I'd been asked to host a fundraiser trivia night for a group of social workers. For the gig I decided to resurrect a character I'd created called Babs Bluett, a tacky, wise-crackin', gum-chewing showbiz singer. I wasn't completely naïve. I was well aware that trivia nights can become ugly affairs in which the nicest people turn into rude, obnoxious arseholes all in the name of raising money for a new set of chairs for a migrant learning centre or some equally deserving cause. The social workers were no exception. I clearly remember standing on the stage in the big echoey town hall asking the question: 'What physical manoeuvre can kangaroos not perform that humans can?' (This would have been about question number five, which meant I only had 995 to go.)

The correct answer is, of course, that kangaroos can't jump backwards. But I sincerely thought the suggestion from one team that kangaroos can't perform oral sex was equally valid so I allowed them the point. All hell broke loose. By the time I got to reading out question number ten, things were getting personal.

'Speak up!'

'We can't hear you!'

'Could you speak clearly?'

'We can't understand you!'

At one point a guy from the audience grabbed my sheet of questions and said, 'Oh, give me the mike, I'll read them out.' And everyone cheered! Maybe if my character hadn't had a lisp …

I left the gig and, in my extremely high-heeled shiny red shoes, walked the three kilometres home, tears flowing from my eyes and milk dripping from my breasts. That was it, I decided, I was never going to perform again.

The point is, John was a juggler in drag and I was an unemployed breastfeeding mother who between us had no money and no financial prospects whatsoever. Yet still the Commonwealth Bank gave us a loan to buy a house. John's parents also gave us some money towards the deposit and so our search began.

On this particular Saturday morning we had one week to go before we had to get out of our rental house, no pressure or anything. We were on our way to look at another house when we passed a red *Auction Here Today* flag. We pulled up. We spent a couple of minutes walking through the house and came back out the front just as the auction was starting.

'Should I bid?' John asked me.

'Sure,' I replied.

Ten minutes later we were first-time home-owners. We signed the papers, got back in our car and drove away. Barely a minute passed before I burst into tears. John pulled the car over.

'Scotty, what's the matter?'

'I hate it.'

'You hate what?'

'The house. I absolutely hate it.'

John looked shocked. 'Well, why did you tell me to bid?'

'Because we have to live somewhere and I knew all we could afford was some ugly, horrible, depressing piece of shit.'

But you adapt; and for every negative there is a positive.

Negative to positive number one

We were so exhausted and emotionally drained from moving into a place that was so much worse than anything we'd ever rented that we became extremely accident-prone. On the positive side — and this is a big positive; in fact I would go so far as to say that this positive was in fact a blessed miracle — I became pregnant again and nine months later our daughter was born. All children like to believe they are conceived in loving circumstances and, as I once explained to Bonnie, 'Of course you were conceived in love. It's just that John and I have no recollection of where or when that loving event took place.' It was indeed a complete mystery.

'Scotty, do you think it could have happened when we were staying at my folks' place, you know, when we were in between houses? Maybe we were that tired and had a bit to drink ...'

'I don't know, John, I just don't know.'

Negative to positive number two

Our roof leaked. Badly. Very badly. On the positive side, our kids grew up believing that it was perfectly normal for a family to wear raincoats *inside* the house. An added bonus was that one day when John's folks came to visit, there happened to be a terrible storm and water was flowing through our hallway. John's mum, an independently wealthy woman, immediately offered us a no-interest loan of $5000 to get the roof fixed.

Negative to positive number three

We had an outdoor toilet situated at the furthest corner of the backyard. Our dismayed friends would carry on, 'You've only got an outdoor toilet? What do you do when you need to do wee in the middle of the night?' I would simply reply, 'Well, that's when having a bathtub comes in handy.' On the positive side, the outside toilet was a God-given gift first thing in the morning, when John always displayed a very robust and, shall we say, free and relaxed attitude to releasing his bodily toxins.

Negative to positive number four

In one room the walls were covered in a thick, rough stucco plaster. One wall featured a massive crack that extended from floor to ceiling. The advantage was that this crack was in the shape of Africa, which made it very easy, when discussing Nelson Mandela and issues of apartheid for instance, to put the situation into a geographical context.

Negative to positive number five

Now that we had a mortgage and one income, we were broke. After paying the essential bills there was nothing left over, and I really do mean nothing. On the positive side, John and I came to appreciate things more – water, for instance. John's sister Susan had come to stay with us for a few days. At the time she was a free-and-easy single woman, doing well as a psychologist. One night I was on my way to the shops to get some milk. Susan said, 'Oh Scotty, while you're there would you mind picking up a large bottle of fizzy mineral water?'

'Sure, not a problem,' I sang out. But it was a problem. A big problem. I only had enough money for a bottle of milk. Five minutes later John arrived home to find me on the front porch on my hands and knees, looking under our old couch. 'Scotty, what are you doing?'

'I'm looking for some money. I remember dropping some coins here once and I thought there might still be twenty cents under the couch.' I explained the pickle I was in.

'Well, why don't you just tell Susan?' he asked me.

'I can't. I'm too embarrassed.'

Even thick-skinned John agreed that having to admit you don't have enough money for a bottle of water was a little humiliating and so he joined in the search. We went through the kids' toy cupboard, the laundry baskets and my old handbag. Finally John found a fifty-cent piece under the passenger seat of the car. Eureka! It could have been a gold nugget the size of a softball we were that excited. Later that night when we were sipping on a glass of the precious water, John and I raved, 'This water, isn't it tasty? Mmmm ...'

One time our best friends Richard and Fran rang to invite us to a special dinner to celebrate Fran's birthday; we were the only guests. They lived a couple of hours away, in the small country town of Loch. Richard was planning to drive to Melbourne to buy extravagant amounts of fresh, fabulous seafood at the Queen Vic Market. He'd been studying recipe books for a week beforehand and was getting ready to cook up an absolute feast of oysters, prawns, calamari and a whole baked fish. He'd already selected and bought the wines. We were to bring nothing but ourselves and our kids, and we would stay the night with them.

On the day we were to leave for this special dinner, we realised we didn't have enough petrol to get us as far as Loch. And we didn't have the money to buy any. That's when I felt as though I belonged in the novel *Angela's Ashes*. I sat at our laminex kitchen table, put my head in my hands and I wept and wept and wept with self-pity. I felt pathetic. I felt ashamed. I was too embarrassed to tell my great friends that we couldn't come to dinner because we couldn't afford to put petrol in our car.

So I didn't tell them. Instead I went to our phone and, with a steely resolve, picked up the receiver. I dialled Richard and Fran's place. Oh no. Oh my God, no. I couldn't believe it. Our phone had been cut off because we hadn't paid the bill. I fell to the floor in a kind of Bette Davis slump and really howled. Jordie and Bonnie stood nervously nearby and then Jordie quietly asked, 'Are you alright, Mum?' Continuing my Bette Davis performance, I swept them both into my arms, held them tight and whimpered, 'It's alright, kids. It's just that we haven't got any petrol and we haven't got a phone so Mummy's a bit upset, that's all.' I got them into the double pusher and we went to the phone box. (This was pre-mobile phone days.) I rang reverse charges. I spoke to Richard, who had just returned from his seafood shopping expedition in Melbourne.

'Oh sorry, Richard, but we can't come now. Yeah, um ... I'm feeling a bit ... tired, yeah. So we won't be able to make it.'

There was a dreadful silence as Richard absorbed this information. Frostily he said, 'Oh, okay then.' I came back home and continued to weep. Now my best friends thought I just couldn't be bothered coming to their special birthday dinner!

John arrived home. He went straight back to the phone box, rang Richard and Fran and told them the humiliating truth.

'If only you'd told us earlier, we would've lent you the money,' Richard said. I wept at their kindness.

On a positive note, word of our predicament must have spread because soon after the Richard/Fran/no-petrol fiasco I went to our letterbox to find an envelope addressed to us; by its feel and shape it was obviously a card. This was intriguing as it wasn't anyone's birthday. I opened the envelope. The card was decorated with flowers. Inside I read the words, 'Heard things were a bit tough. Hope this helps.' Included was a cheque for $500.

Negative to positive number six

What actually started off as a positive did an about-face and became a clear negative the day it was officially declared a death trap. I loved our open fireplace, which was surrounded by a lovely wooden mantelpiece. Often on cold Melbourne winter nights the four of us would sit around it and freeze because it didn't seem to radiate any heat nor, for that matter, did it burn particularly well (more like a dull, smoky, smouldering situation). But it was a symbol, if not a reality, of warmth and love and cosy family life.

But when we couldn't hear a word anyone was saying because of the chattering of teeth, I finally realised that a metaphor for warmth was no longer adequate; I decided to ring a chimney sweep. To be honest, I didn't even know they still existed until I saw an advertisement in the local paper. I fully expected to see Dick Van Dyke covered in soot, singing 'Chim, chiminee' at the door. As it turned out, a perfectly ordinary young man in overalls arrived and crawled into the fireplace, lying on his back and peering up inside the chimney. After less than a minute he got up and strode over to me, placing both hands on my shoulders. Unnervingly, he just stared at me. Either he's going to murder me or he's going to kiss me passionately, I thought. Looking me straight in the eye, he said, 'You must promise me that you will NEVER, EVER light another fire in that fireplace.'

'Why?'

'Have a look,' he gestured.

I lay on my back inside the fireplace. I was shocked to see that the lovely wooden mantel had in fact been put there to cosmetically cover what had certainly once been a fireplace but was now just a big hole in the wall with no brickwork around it. We'd been lighting a fire with nothing but bare exposed wood in front of it.

The positive side was that we hadn't burnt to death.

Another positive was that we got it fixed for almost nothing. We got a bricklayer to make a brick hearth. It was ugly, but the bricks were free – wink, wink, nudge, nudge, say no more, if you get what I mean. But just in case you *don't* get what I mean, John stole them. Yes, he sneaked off in the middle of a very cold night wearing his op-shop army coat and a hand-knitted woollen beanie and furtively filled the car with a load of brand-new red bricks that he claimed had been sitting at his workplace for months. I waited at home anxiously, feeling a deep connection with Judy Moran as I pictured my partner getting caught red-handed, a flashlight beaming in his face and a cop yelling, 'Just drop the brick, buddy. Drop the fuckin' brick or we'll shoot!'

Just as I'd decided what I would wear to John's funeral – a smart, contemporary black suit with a Jackie Onassis–style hat and a black veil over the face – I heard the family Datsun pull up. I peered out the window. There was something about the car; it looked different. Oh my God, the boot-end was so heavy it was almost touching the ground, forcing the front bonnet to rise up on quite a tilt. He'd done it! John, our Robin Hood, had saved the day. He was going to keep his family warm, even if it meant someone else couldn't quite finish their backyard paving.

Negative to positive number seven

The garage was an enormous, ugly, aluminium structure that took up half the backyard. Sure, I'm the first to admit that this garage might've been a real asset and may even have come in handy if you'd been able to, let's say, drive a car into it. But this was out of the question because it turned out our driveway was not our driveway after all. It was, in fact, a public laneway that the council had sold to our neighbours prior to auction and they had since closed it off. It's not as if anyone bothered to inform us, so how were we to know that our driveway had been sold? Who'd have thought to ask, 'Oh, and by the way, you see that driveway, the one running straight into our garage? Is that ours?'

On the positive side – and I must stress that this has been a positive for the rest of the family and a personal nightmare for me – the garage became known as the 'big cupboard'.

Negative to positive number eight

During the buying and moving in to number 26, John developed alopecia. He would lose whole sections of his thick dark hair, leaving bald patches the size of fifty-cent pieces all over his head. It was when he started to lose his thick dark eyebrows that it really became noticeable. First it was only the middle section of his right eyebrow that went, but then the whole half of his left eyebrow disappeared. Because he was a clown, people would laugh and say things like, 'I love what you've done to your eyebrows, John. You look hysterical!' To which John would explain that it was alopecia and much awkwardness would follow.

On the positive side, when John had only one half of an eyebrow left – and even it was starting to fall out – his mother took me aside and said, 'About that $5000 you owe me for the roof repairs – forget it. I don't want John to lose any more of his hair.'

CHAPTER 2
The phone call

t's quite possible that John and I might never have stayed together and had children if it wasn't for a phone call I received in the early hours of 27 August 1983.

It's not that John and I had never discussed having kids; in fact, we rather liked the idea. But we were baby boomers, part of the 'me' generation. We didn't want to be trapped by a mortgage man, we didn't want a nine-to-five job killing our creativity. We wanted to be free-spirited bohemian types, always open to life's adventures, who could really stick it to the man by wearing a pair of tights and a tie-dyed shirt to conservative family gatherings.

John and I first met near the banks of the Murray River way back in the days when water was free, sprinklers were always turned on in suburban backyards,

17

and rivers flowed like ... well, they flowed like rivers. It was 1981 and we were two of the five new recruits who'd arrived in downtown Albury to become part of the Murray River Performing Group's Clown Ensemble.

I'll never forget the first moment I clapped eyes on John. He swept into clown headquarters on a pair of rollerskates, a silver banjo ukulele slung over his shoulder. He was wearing a white cotton shirt that had lost all its buttons, revealing a beautiful, strong, tanned torso. His big, baggy, old blue shorts were held in place by a green and white spotted tie which he was using as a belt. His legs were muscular from years of pushbike riding; he didn't own a car. His dark, wild mane of hair was pulled back to expose a silver stud of a blowfly in his ear. His teeth, flashing in one of the broadest grins I'd ever seen, were straight and white. To be honest, I found it quite disturbing to see someone so happy. I was immediately suspicious. (I've since tried to replicate his smile and it's so wide it hurts. I've also tried over the years to break him down and expose his happiness as a fraud. But after twenty-six years of consistent effort, I'm forced to admit that his happiness may indeed be the real deal.)

That first day, once all the clowns had met one another, it was agreed that we would go free clowning that night. For those not quite familiar with clown-speak, free clowning is when you head off into a crowd and do your own thing, be it juggling, funny walks, a slapstick routine, balloon animals, et cetera. Since the famous children's Flying Fruit Fly Circus was performing in town that night, we decided to go and do our own thing outside their main tent. As the clown ensemble's director explained, 'It'll give us a chance to check one another out and get to see what we all do.'

In no time at all, John had whisked three balls out of his backpack which he proceeded to juggle, accompanying himself on kazoo, which he also just happened to have handy. Next thing, he was balancing a broomstick on his nose. Oh Christ, where did this guy get his energy from, not to mention his skills? And what about his confidence? I felt sick to my stomach. I was burning with the humiliation that I knew was totally inevitable.

I'd lied. I'd lied big time to get the job. When I say I lied, I mean that I kind of implied I could juggle. The truth was I was terrified of balls. On the rare occasion that someone at school had attempted to throw me a basketball, I had simply screamed in fright and run in the opposite direction. As for stilt-walking, forget it; I have a problem with heights. And as for being able to do the odd back-flip: I once signed up for private acrobatic classes with the late Mickey Ashton (of Ashton circus fame). He strapped me into the leather harness and as he pulled on the rope I went up into the air. It was then that I started hyperventilating. Mickey called to me, 'Are you okay?'

'Not really,' I replied. 'I think I need to come down.'

'Scotty, you're only a metre off the ground,' he said. He then yanked on the rope and before I knew it I'd done my back-flip. Well, almost. I pretty much landed on my head. It was at this point that Mickey informed me, 'There are some people, not many but there are some, who should never attempt acrobatics, and Scotty, you're one of them.' So why the hell did I join the Murray River Performing Group's Clown Ensemble? Because there were no positions left in their acting troupe.

Somehow I got through that first day and began to love my life as a totally dysfunctional clown. About a month after that first meeting, John and I were at the same party. We acknowledged a mutual attraction, went home together and let's just say there were four feet poking out the end of my bed that night.

Two years later, John and I left Albury and moved into a share-house in Northcote, Melbourne. It was the first time we had ever lived together. A few weeks had passed in fairly blissful circumstances when one morning, quite out of the blue, John rolled over to face me in bed and announced, 'I'm thinking of going overseas.'

'When?'

'Soon.'

'How soon?'

'In a month maybe.'

I couldn't believe it. We'd just moved in together and now he wanted to go away on his own.

'Don't you see, Scotty?'

'No.'

'It's because we now live together that I know I've got

to go away, because I now know without a doubt that I love living with you.'

Well, gee, that cleared things up.

He went on to explain that now that he knew without doubt that he wanted to spend the rest of his life with me, before he did so he felt he needed to go to Italy.

'... and have sex with some hot Italian chicks before you settle down?'

'No, Scotty. I want to check out the street theatre and community festivals they have there.'

As John continued to rave on about the exciting festivals that he'd obviously been researching, I lay next to him in seething silence, imagining the long, shapely, olive-skinned legs of the exquisitely beautiful, talented, highly sexed street performer John would inevitably meet while he was away. I was sure her name would be Angelica or something equally alluring. But hang on, oh my God ...

'John, you can't go away.'

'Why not?'

'Our bed. How am I going to roll it up? I can't do it on my own.'

The 'bed' was the futon mattress we'd just purchased to celebrate moving in together. At the time, futons were relatively new in Australia and were made of thick, heavy cotton wadding, which meant the king-size version, the one John and I had bought, weighed approximately two and a half tonnes. The young Japanese salesman was very helpful and suggested we buy the wooden slat base to go with it. We just peered at him incredulously and told him of our plans to have our mattress on the floor. He looked very serious and explained in no uncertain terms, 'If you put a king-size, cotton wadding–filled futon straight onto the floor, you have to be prepared to get up every morning – and I mean every morning – and roll up the mattress so it can breathe. Do you understand me? It needs to breathe. It needs to air. If you don't roll it up every day it will sweat. It will get damp. That is why you need to roll it up every day, I mean EVERY SINGLE DAY. Do you understand what I'm saying?'

Yeah, yeah, alright, calm down, keep your pants on, buddy. We hear you. We need to roll up the mattress every day. Check. Understood. Roger, over and out. God, I'd heard the pressure on workers in Japan was fierce but come on, we were in a mattress shop in Melbourne, no need to get all *hari-kiri* about the situation.

We paid for the mattress but before our departure the sales guy grimaced, 'Um, look, how can I say this? I just get the feeling that you're ...' He paused and tried starting again. 'Look, I get the sense that maybe you might not be the sort of people ... um ... well, you strike me as ... how can I say this? You strike me as free sort of people, um ... very relaxed, laidback ...' He laughed uncomfortably. We just looked at him. It crossed my mind that perhaps he might want to buy some dope or something. 'What I'm trying to say is that maybe you two won't want to roll up a mattress every morning. Maybe you should seriously think about getting a base.'

Talk about pushy. Didn't he understand? For people like us, rolling up a mattress every morning had a primitive tribal feel to it. It wasn't a chore; it was a creative expression of our freedom. It would give us room to do our yoga!

'Oh, so you do yoga?'

'No, we don't. But you never know. One day we might.' The salesman looked mystified.

The next day, our futon was delivered. It took two huge removal chaps, both of whom looked as though they regularly consumed a tub of steroids for breakfast, to carry it in. That night John and I unrolled our king-size mattress onto the linoleum floor and spent the night convincing ourselves that we loved that it was as hard as a compacted Australian paddock after eighteen years of drought.

As promised, the next morning we dutifully rolled up the mattress again. But by the second morning the novelty had well and truly worn off. I mean for God's sake, we had to find somewhere to put our doona and pillows, not to mention that, yes, sure, it could be made into the shape of a couch, but we already had a couch in our lounge room; why would we sit on a couch in our bedroom? Certainly, you could always sit on it and read a book, which is exactly what I had to do that first afternoon because I couldn't do what I love to do, which is lie down on my bed and read, because the bed was rolled up into a couch.

And so it happened that after that first night, John and I didn't get around to rolling up the futon for a week ... or maybe two. But so what? What could possibly happen?

Mould! That's what. Big patches of disgusting, greenish-grey mould growing all over the base of the mattress. As a result we now had to get it into the backyard, to get some sunshine onto what now resembled a giant slab of blue-vein cheese. We tried to lift it but it was impossibly heavy. John then devised an ingenious method, which called on all his skills as a circus performer. Firstly, he positioned himself at one end of the futon. He then did a deep forward bend and, stretching both his arms out sideways, he grabbed the end of the mattress in both hands. He then proceeded to do a complete forward roll, taking the mattress with him so that he ended up back on his feet, his head touching his knees, the mattress now completely covering him. Since he was unable to see a thing, it was my job to clear the hallway of obstacles so that John could propel himself forward and head straight out the back door unimpeded.

'You can't go overseas John. I won't be able to roll up the bed. And you know what that means? It will become completely covered in mould and fungus and when you come back — if you come back — there I'll be, just lying here in this bed with a wracking, gurgling, phlegm-filled cough, with nothing to eat but the crop of mushrooms that will have grown all around me.'

'Scotty, if it's the last thing I do, I'll make you a wooden slat base before I go.'

And true to his word, it was pretty much the last thing John did do before boarding the plane for New Delhi. Two days before his departure, John went to a timber yard where he purchased the wood. 'Gee, it was cheap.' Such simple words.

At approximately one o'clock the following morning, John feverishly began sawing, hammering, drilling and nailing, making the bed-base on site, in our bedroom.

Our housemates soon emerged from their bedrooms looking bleary-eyed and quite deranged. 'What the fuck are you doing, John?'

'Building a Japanese bed-base.'

I timidly enquired, 'John, how do you know what to do?'

'Instinct, Scotty.'

Later that day, after a night of very little sleep, a friend we'd worked with in the clown ensemble called in for a visit. Mark was a big man, a really big man. Now when I say big, I don't mean fat. I mean tall and broad and solid and strong. John took Mark into our bedroom to proudly show off his handiwork. In a crazy, spontaneous, fun-loving tribute to our days in the clown troupe, Mark took a run at the bed and threw himself on it, landing flat on his back. We heard a series of dramatic, gut-wrenching cracks. Mark stood up and we rolled back the mattress. At least a quarter of the slats had snapped. 'Well, I guess that's why the wood was cheap,' John shrugged. He devised an ingenious solution which involved placing single bricks and a small piece of wood under each of the broken slats. 'Just a temporary measure, Scotty. I'll fix it when I get back.'

A couple of months after John flew away, the show I'd been performing in ended its run and I decided to join him in Rome. The flight seemed to take forever and I was in customs for years, but finally I emerged through those double doors, and there waiting in the arrivals lounge was …

Oh my God, oh Jesus, what on earth? It wasn't so much that John was a skeletal shadow of his former robust self (a consequence of having sipped a drop of unboiled water in India) nor was it the funny haircut, kind of shaved at the sides and long and wild on top; no, it was the moustache that threw me. I couldn't believe it. I was absolutely repulsed. It was a tiny Hitler moustache. He offered me the single, wilted red rose he was holding. I took it in my hand, all the while just staring at him, wondering if it was too soon to announce that the relationship was over. Sure, it was a little inconvenient to have come all the way to the other side of the world for this realisation but hey, life's like that: strange and mysterious and sometimes extremely impractical.

John must have picked up on the vibe, which wouldn't have been hard considering I was making comments like, 'I just can't bear to look at you.' Later that day he emerged from the bathroom sans facial hair and we proceeded with our holiday.

John continued in his dogged quest to experience street theatre festivals. We would inevitably arrive in a small, out-of-the-way Italian village, only to find that the festival had already happened, or wasn't happening until the following week, or only took place every alternate year and guess what, this wasn't the right year; or in some places the festival was cancelled altogether because ... well, 'just because' was usually the most detailed explanation. The one festival we did make it to required us to pitch our two-man tent on an Italian soccer ground and bake in the intense heat of the Italian summer, camping alongside thousands of Italian hippies. Whether it was Byron Bay in Australia or a small village in Italy, I couldn't help but conclude that bongo-playing hippies gave me the shits. But the Italian hippies gave me more than that. They gave John and me the worst case of tinea we'd ever had. Be warned: if ever you find yourself in a stinking makeshift camping ground where the heat is putrid and the people even more so (albeit in a spiritual, sweat-soaked, Zen kind of way) and you have to make use of a communal shower in the local soccer club, for goodness sake WEAR THONGS. Alternatively, you could just go to Venice, stay in a comfy hotel and take a ride in a gondola like normal tourists do.

From there, John and I took our disgusting, itching feet south to Sicily. We arrived to find that yes, we were there at the right time for the festival, but it had just been cancelled due to a hastily called election. So we then moved our tinea to a small seaside village where you could get into an elevator at the top of a huge cliff, travel down through solid rock and, when the doors opened at the bottom, find yourself on a small rocky beach where you could swim in the cooling blue waters of the something-or-other sea (I'm not one for geographical details). Of an evening we would eat exquisite seafood at a small hotel at the top of the cliff. The fish was cheap and freshly caught by the local Sicilian fisherman, Salvatore. A beautiful, suntanned, lean and muscular man, Salvatore befriended John and me, taking us under his wing, showing us the sights in his boat, and telling us the history of the place.

One day, when John was off elsewhere, Salvatore took me to a beautiful olive grove and propositioned me. That's right, he wanted to know if I would make love to him right there and then. And by God, it has to be said I certainly contemplated the idea. The situation had that air of seizing the moment, of doing something wild, something crazy, and no one would ever have to know. Think of it: a screwed-up, stitched-up, guilt-ridden, ex-Catholic girl loses herself in a wild, sexual frenzy with a young, peasant fisherman in a luxuriant, green Sicilian field underneath an extra-virgin olive oil tree. I'd like to be able to say that at this point I thought of John but in truth I was thinking only of my tinea-covered feet. How would I ever explain to this fisherman why I had to make love wearing my walking boots?

As we were spending a good deal of time with Salvatore, I decided to tell John of our encounter in the olive grove. John was cool about it. Turns out Salvatore had propositioned him too.

John and I had been back from overseas for about a week when the phone rang at 4 am.

'Hello?'

'Denise …'

'Mum, what's wrong?'

'It's your dad, he's in the hospital. It's not good.'

That last sentence – 'It's not good' – turned out to be Mum's way of telling me that Dad had died of a sudden heart attack. He was fifty-nine years old.

What I experienced in those moments following the phone call was more than shock and grief at the loss of my dad, who I simply adored. I had a sort of out of body experience where I witnessed my chest being torn open in a Sigourney Weaver, *Aliens*-type moment. There was no blood, no pain, just a clean tear like the ripping of a strong fabric and out of my chest a small bird escaped and flew away. I realised that the bird was the carefree, irresponsible, childlike part of my spirit. It flew away, never to reappear in quite the same way.

At this exact moment I was forced to do something I'd never wanted to do: I had to grow up. And so, at twenty-eight years of age, I stopped being the 'baby' of the family and assumed responsibility for looking after Mum. My sister had just given birth to her second child and lived a long way from our parents' house; I had no children and lived nearby. So I was the one who stayed with Mum that night. When she asked me to sleep with her, quite frankly the shock nearly took me out with my very own heart attack; Mum and I weren't even into hugging each other at Christmas time. I wore one of Mum's nighties and tentatively lay beside her in the same spot that my larger-than-life, happy-go-lucky dad had been sleeping the night before. My mum faced away from me. I took a deep breath, told myself to be brave and curled around her.

The other wake-up call from that phone call was to remind me that life is short. If you want to do something, you can't muck around. So the very next day I said to John, 'I want to have children now.'

The problem was I didn't think I could. I didn't know for sure but I'd been told by a gynaecologist by the name of Dr Pill – I swear it's the truth – that I had a bicornuate uterus (a heart shape instead of a pear shape) which meant it was unlikely I could carry a baby full term; he suggested I would probably miscarry at about eighteen to twenty weeks. Not the cheeriest news to hear when you're a young woman, but there was hope. I could try having my womb reconstructed and it may then do its job. Mum's phone call forced me to pull my head out and finally face whether I could have children or not.

I booked in to see a womb reconstructer, a very nice chap, who suggested that before I had surgery I should go home and try to have a baby first. Good God, I never even considered such an option! Pretty much nine months later, I was lying in a hospital bed breastfeeding our son Jordie.

'Scotty, isn't it great to know we can have children?' John beamed. I nodded in a dazed, shell-shocked kind of way.

A brief history of heart attacks in the Scott family

At four years old, I was sitting on the back step of Nanna Scott's house in West Heidelberg, reading books with my sister. My nanna was walking back up the path from the Hills hoist, where she'd been hanging up some clothes. As far as I could gather it was the biggest Hills hoist in the world; it had to be because Nanna had nine children. Nanna squeezed between me and my sister and headed into the kitchen. She called out, 'What do you want on your sandwich, Denise, vegemite or peanut butter?' I leaned back and looked at her through the kitchen door. And then she dropped dead. Just like that, she fell to the floor. I never had time to tell her, 'Vegemite, Nanna, vegemite.' Like Dad, she was fifty-nine years old.

Uncle Len, Uncle Frank, Uncle Doug, Aunty Edna, Russ – they all had or have bad tickers. Once, at a family funeral, my Aunty Edna placed her hands on my shoulders and fixed me with a stern stare. Standing there, eyeball to eyeball, big breast to even bigger breast, she said to me, 'Denise, you are such a Scott. You must promise me here and now that if you ever, and I mean *ever*, think you've got indigestion, get yourself to emergency straight away because it will be a heart attack for sure. Do you promise?'

'I promise.'

On the other side of the family, my mum has had three heart attacks and her own mother died of a heart attack when she was in her late fifties.

I have warned my family on many occasions, 'Make the most of me kids, I mightn't be around for long.'

CHAPTER 3
A number of rash decisions

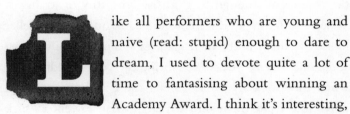ike all performers who are young and naive (read: stupid) enough to dare to dream, I used to devote quite a lot of time to fantasising about winning an Academy Award. I think it's interesting, and says a lot about Australia's self-esteem issues, that I never ever dreamed about winning a Logie. Not once. No, I always saw myself on the red carpet wearing a fabulous Versace gown, my orthodontically enhanced, perfect white teeth gleaming for the cameras. My co-star Richard Gere would be positively falling about, laughing at my warm larrikin charm while simultaneously smitten by my girl-down-under, bronzed, blonde, natural beauty. And as I made my acceptance speech for Best Actress in a Motion Picture, knowing that everyone back home would be crying with pride that their little Aussie girl had

hit the big time, I would know that this was the night I would finally succumb to passion and go back to Richard's place, make mad passionate love and decide to spend the rest of my life with him.

But in reality, here I was at number 26 with John and two small children. I had completely relinquished the Hollywood fantasy and replaced it with another. I began to fantasise about winning a Nobel Prize for finding a cure for eczema. This could have had something to do with the fact that my children were covered in it. Let's get this clear: they weren't so bad that they had to be hospitalised but they were bad enough to gain the sympathy of strangers. When I took them with me to the bank one day, the teller looked at them both, then glanced sympathetically at me and said, 'Aren't you brave, bringing your children out when they look like that!' Then there was the one and only time I put them into daycare: when I went to pick them up they were both covered in scratches and blood. The childcare workers were distraught. 'We're so sorry,' they said, 'but we just didn't know what to do.'

And I'll never forget our trip to Darwin. The children were toddlers – Bonnie would have been about one and Jordie two and a half – and we all flew up there to see John, who was performing at the Bougainvillea Festival with the Essendon Policewomen's Marching Band. That plane trip from Melbourne to Darwin was the longest six hours of my life. The atmospheric conditions onboard seemed to aggravate the kids' skin. The further we flew, the worse it got and I had to try to stroke both of them as they scratched and became redder and rawer and bloodier as time went on. The hardest thing to deal with was the family sitting directly across the aisle from us – they were perfect. There was the really attractive mum, with perfect hair and perfect make-up (the fact that any young mum had the time or energy or self-esteem to apply make-up was a complete enigma to me) sitting next to the handsome dad with a beautiful smile, olive skin and expensive, tasteful clothes that appeared to have been ironed. Then there was the gorgeous little daughter with thick, blonde curly hair and yes, of course, creamy white skin and rose-petal cheeks. And the son who, like his dad, had olive skin, dark-brown eyes and long, thick lashes. And didn't the air hostesses love them! They gave them colouring books and pencils and lollies. They took them to the cockpit and offered to escort them to the toilet so the parents could have a break. Oh, those air hostesses couldn't get enough of laughing and playing and singing with those kids. Meanwhile, the more my kids began to resemble something out of the *X-Files*, the more the air hostesses ignored us. In retrospect, I think they may have been frightened; by the end of the trip they weren't even able to look at us. They'd walk down the aisle chatting away to people, checking if they wanted anything: 'A cup of tea perhaps, sir?' or 'Could I get you a pillow, madam?' But as they approached us they would look the other way and kind of run straight past with a distinct sense of urgency and panic. And I'm sure I heard the word 'bubonic' being whispered as I struggled up the aisle to take the kids to the toilet.

Not long after we arrived in Darwin, we were walking down the main street when a local woman took one look at Bonnie's face, screamed, fell down on her knees and started praying.

Rob, a work colleague of John's in Darwin, formed a terrific bond with Bonnie. They played a game where he would say, 'monster face' and they would both make a scary face and Bonnie would just laugh and laugh. We were at a Darwin festival function one evening; I was holding Bonnie in my arms and talking to a woman I'd never met before. Rob appeared in the room and made a beeline for us. He looked at Bonnie and said, 'Hey, monster face.' Choking on her wine, the horrified woman glared at Rob in disbelief. I mean okay, the kid's face was covered in welts, but to call her monster face! Rob made a feeble attempt to explain but to do so properly would've meant referring to Bonnie's eczema and … oh well, it was easier just to chalk it up as one of life's embarrassing moments.

Another time, I went to visit an old friend (and I use the word 'friend' loosely). Taking one look at my kids, she immediately started raving, 'Oh, my hairdresser had eczema as a child. In fact, he had it all over his face just like your daughter.'

'And how does he look now?'

'Fucked. His face is absolutely fucked, covered in scars from all the scratching.'

Poor little Bonn! Because the eczema was on her face she looked so much worse than Jordie. The white mesh sides of her portable cot were permanently smeared with blood from rubbing her cheeks on them to try to get some relief. She had no hair or eyebrows because of the scratching and rubbing. Her eyes were puffed and swollen because it was also on her eyelids.

Meanwhile my mum would ring and ask, 'Denise, do you think there's any chance of getting a pixie photo of Bonnie? She's the only grandchild I haven't got on the lounge-room wall.'

'Yeah, sure, Mum, I'll get that done soon.'

'Well, you'd better get a move on. I want it to match the other kids' photos and they were all about six months old when they had theirs taken.'

Of course, I was waiting for Bonnie's skin to clear but time was running out. Finally, when Bonnie was nearly eight months old, I saw it advertised that the pixie photo man was due to appear at our local Kmart; I knew what I had to do. I put Bonnie in her best dress, popped her in the pusher and headed to the store. We waited in the pixie photo queue and, when we were two babies away from photo time, I knelt down in front of Bonnie and brazenly produced a cosmetics bag from under the pusher. Acting as though it was a perfectly normal thing to do, I then began covering Bonnie's face with some of my stage make-up — a thick pancake base applied with a specially made sea sponge. Then I gave her just a touch of blush and then I thought, well, look, while I'm here I may as well ... and that's when I drew on some eyebrows.

Each night, John and I would sleep in our king-size bed with a child on either side of us. John was in charge of Jordie, I was in charge of Bonnie. John would stroke Jordie's skin and apply whatever naturopathic concoction we were trying at the time, and I would stroke Bonnie. We did not get a full night's sleep, nor, for that matter, more than three hours' consecutive sleep, for over four years.

So that's why I became obsessed with finding a cure for eczema. In the spirit of hippiedom, we resolutely refused to use cortisone. We tried all sorts of alternative remedies, including a pill the size of a surfboard from a naturopath who told us it had to be placed under the small child's tongue and kept there until it dissolved some ten to fifteen minutes later. If it wasn't already perfectly clear that this woman had never had a child, she then went on to stress that we had to put the tablet under the tongue 'without using your hands. We don't want your hands contaminating the pill, do we?' What were we meant to do? Place the tablet under our small child's tongue using a mini pair of sterile tongs held between our teeth? Or there was the homeopath who sent us home with a questionnaire the size of a phone book, which included questions like, 'When did you get your first tooth?' How the hell was my teething history going to help cure my kids' eczema? Oh, and in another section we had to give our academic history, including whether we'd done Year 12 and what our results were. What was that about? Was there research to show that women who got a C for Year 12 French had an 85 per cent greater chance of producing children with skin problems?

But perhaps all this was written in the stars. About a year before I met John I'd gone to a fortune-teller. He had an afro hairdo, wore a cream-coloured caftan, and sat at a table in the sparsely furnished lounge room of his small one-bedroom flat. He didn't even have a ball to gaze into. I was single at the time and there was no sign of love coming my way. I needed some answers to some worrying questions about life. 'Will I have children?'

He looked down at the bare table, explaining that he was able to pick up 'vibes'. 'You will have three children,' he said in a reverential tone.

My eyes lit up for a second. Then they dimmed as I asked in a pathetic, whimpering, I-dare-not-dream-for-too-much sort of voice, 'Will there be a father involved?'

Afro man said, 'Well, there usually is,' at which point he paused tactfully, leaving the words 'you dickhead' unspoken.

'What I mean,' I continued, tactfully leaving the words 'Afro man' unspoken, 'is will there be, you know, a guy that's going to, you know … be, I don't know, kind of there?'

I got no response from that big circle of hair. So I got more specific. 'Will these children have the same father and will he be actively involved in their upbringing?'

He mumbled that he couldn't give me those details but then, without looking up, he went on to announce that these children 'will all definitely have skin problems'. At least he was able to be sure about something.

I recalled this event during my pregnancies and wondered whether I hadn't inadvertently convinced myself and my babies, via the umbilical cord, that we did indeed have a prophecy to fulfil. Oh, and about that third child: of course this never happened; but hey, at fifty-three – and I'm not bragging, just stating the facts – it's still a possibility.

Eventually, John and I took the kids to an allergy clinic. They were tested and between the two of them they were found to be allergic to wheat, most meats, yeast, dairy products, sugar, eggs, most fruits, most common vegetables, chocolate, fish and nuts. Jordie and Bonnie were even allergic to alcohol! This was relevant as my daily ritual at the time was to turn on the telly at 5.30, watch *Perfect Match*, have a glass of chardonnay and breastfeed Bonnie. But now she was allergic to the wine that was being passed on via my breast milk so sadly I had to give up that little ritual – the breastfeeding, not the alcohol. (Joke: of course I gave up the alcohol.) In fact, the kids and I gave up eating; well, we had to. Evidently, there was nothing we could eat except grass and cardboard. In reality, we did indeed have to stop eating virtually anything we'd previously known. Put it this way, if it wasn't grey, flavourless and drab with the texture of a rubber thong, we knew we couldn't touch it.

I became devoted to experimenting and cooking things we could eat, such as adzuki bean pilau and rice-flour pancakes with … well, with nothing on top, unless you wanted to throw on the leftover adzuki bean pilau. Once I made an allergy-free cake featuring pumpkin and buckwheat flour. I was thrilled with it − at last I had baked something that tasted good, something I could even serve to friends. So I did exactly that, offering a piece to a chap who also happened to be a chef. Looking at me curiously, he said, 'Scotty, do you honestly think this tastes alright?'

I nodded.

'Then you're fuckin' desperate, Scotty, that's all I can say.'

But Bonnie's allergy cake for her second birthday was a triumph, albeit an accidental one. 'Mmm,' the other mums at playgroup murmured before one of them tentatively asked, 'So, what sort of birthday cake can you make without eggs, wheat, milk, butter, cream, sugar or eggs?' I soon found out the answer − a really shithouse one.

Speaking as someone who'd always prided herself on good cakes, it killed me to stand outside our lounge-room door and hear the excited squeals of the kids as our extended family and friends enthused wildly, 'Hey kids! Are you ready to sing happy birthday? The birthday cake is coming. The birthday cake is coming!'

And look, it could be a distorted memory but I'm pretty sure that as I entered the room holding that big, grey brick of demoralisation into which we'd managed to drill some candles, everyone fell into a kind of shocked silence before a few people started a hesitant rendition of 'Happy Birthday'. Unfortunately this progressed into a really rousing, rollicking, way-too-jolly version of 'For She's a Jolly Good Lassie'. It was a sure indication to me that everyone was feeling really sorry for us, having two kids covered in eczema and consequently having to make such awful cakes; and oh, weren't they all so lucky that they had children with perfect skin and no allergies. I could've wept and I would have if it hadn't been for the miracle that saved the day.

At the time I was quietly begging John, 'Please do not cut the cake.' I'd been hoping to just casually remove it from sight. But John, being the eternal Mr Happy Pants, cut it into slices and handed a piece to each child. This was when it became clear that not only did the cake have the look and texture of gum Arabic rubber, but it also tasted like it. And this was when the miracle happened. I don't know which child discovered that if you rolled your piece of cake into a ball and dropped it, it bounced. I mean *really* bounced. I mean it bounced like the old super balls. But pretty soon the house was filled with gleeful kids' laughter as they sent their rolled-up balls of cake boi-oi-oinging all over the house. 'It just goes to show, Scotty,' John said, 'you can always bounce back from tragedy.'

I looked at him with no joy whatsoever and sighed deeply. 'John, I don't want to put a dampener on your joke but the rule in showbiz is: Tragedy plus time equals comedy, time being the crucial word here.'

Not only was our diet restricted but we had to rotate the food so that we could, for instance, only eat adzuki bean pilau every third day or something like that. I had to keep a daily diary recording everything we ate and how the kids' skin reacted. I had a sticker system. A gold star meant a day free of scratching. There were not many of these. It was while I was recording these details that my dream of winning the Nobel Prize took shape. If I couldn't achieve fame from my acting, I'd achieve it by giving something great to the world – the cure for eczema. I could still wear great clothes, something that said gorgeous but humble; I'd be in all the magazines; and my Nobel Prize speech would be an absolute showstopper – emotionally moving but also a complete crack-up.

Being on such a restricted diet meant we couldn't eat anywhere but at home unless we took prepared food with us. Good old Mum, who loved cooking for us and desperately wanted to give John and me a break, invited us for dinner one night. She thought the diet was crazy but respected our attempts so she cooked us an allergy-free meal – except for the gravy which she'd poured on before I could scream, 'NO Mum! For Christ's sake, not gravy! There's wheat in the flour.' I didn't have the heart to say anything, so we ate the meal.

We had an appointment to see the allergy man the following week. He asked about the kids' skin. I explained that it hadn't been great, that they were itching quite a lot. The fact was their skin wasn't any worse than usual but he asked in a rather pointed way whether we'd eaten anything that may have triggered a reaction. I explained about the gravy.

'Mmm,' he took a deep, self-important breath, exhaled, and declared that in future I would have to ask my mother not to use wheat flour in her gravy.

'I can't do that,' I said. 'My mother wouldn't know how to make gravy without ordinary flour.'

He then fixed me in a stare and simply stated, 'Then you won't be able to go to your mother's place for tea again.'

I looked at him for a second before I began to sob inconsolably. (Maybe I was consolable but how would I know? Mr Allergy man did nothing to try to comfort me.) What an unfeeling, sanctimonious … oh, I'm desperately trying to think of an alternative word to arsehole … but I can't. Was there a crueller thing this specialist could ask of a tired mother of two exhausted eczema babies whose mother offered the relief of a weekly home-cooked meal? Was he really saying that a tablespoon of wheat flour was going to completely destroy the lives of my children? Yes, tragically, that's exactly what he was saying.

It was around this time, while I was shopping with the kids, that the checkout chick at the supermarket leaned over to me and suggested in a very caring voice, 'Look, it's none of my business but have you ever thought of taking your children to see a doctor or something?'

We persisted with that allergy diet for over a year. We gave it our best shot and it didn't work. Some years later I co-wrote a comedy sketch with comedian Jean Kittson for an ABC show called *The Big Gig*. We were two mums chatting over a fence. In this particular sketch I was talking about one of my kids having eczema and how we'd taken him off 'all meat, wheat, yeast, dairy, vegetables, fruit, nuts, and yes, his skin looks good but Jesus he's thin! Still, looks good for a kid in a coma.'

The big shift in our lives came when John's sister Susan asked the extended Lane family to Adelaide for Christmas at her house. 'I can't do this, John. I cannot stay at your sister's place and spend four days with your entire family and have my children covered in eczema. We are going to the doctor's and we are going to get some cortisone.'

And that's what we did. When the GP asked if we'd prefer weak cortisone, I said, 'No, give me the strongest you've got and give me a bucket of the stuff.' We applied it to our children's poor, tender skin. Within two days all the symptoms had disappeared. Sure, as soon as we stopped using the cream the eczema would return, but for now it was gone and, most importantly, for the first time in our kids' lives they could sleep through the night.

That first evening at Susan's house, we all squashed into a double bed, which was much higher off the ground than our king-size futon at home. We were all so tired from years of no sleep that we happily drifted off into a deep slumber. Suddenly I was awoken by a thud. I looked over the edge of the bed to see that Bonnie had rolled out and landed on the polished floorboards. She was so tired she hadn't woken up. And I was so tired I left her there.

CHAPTER 4

Normans to the rescue

s I've often been heard to say, 'Thank God the kids had eczema. If it hadn't been for those red, raw bleeding sores I may never have decided to stay at home and discover the joys of being a full-time mum. Come to think of it, I probably would have accepted that role in *When Harry Met Sally*; God knows Billy Crystal was putting on the pressure. As it turned out, Meg Ryan went on to become a Hollywood star and good luck to her; I went on to make homemade playdough, so it turned out well for both of us.

Eczema wasn't the only reason I became a full-time mum. I had a strong belief that the greatest gift I could give to my children – apart from love, food, a Hello Kitty handbag and Mutant Ninja Turtle sword – was time. Having time to mooch is one of life's great treasures; it

47

wasn't only good for the kids, but it was good for me too: a win–win situation. Starting one's day with no plans whatsoever, aside from a vague notion that you might make a pot of stock using a couple of lamb shanks, was as close as I'd ever come to experiencing total bliss. Then again, being able to sit down every weekday at 5.30 pm, pour my first glass of chardonnay and watch *Perfect Match* while the kids ran their own frenzied cut-and-paste session also took me pretty close to nirvana. And the kids flourished in an environment where there was no pressure to do anything – no classes in how to paint like Van Gogh by the age of four, to speak basic French aged two, or to play piano, drums and trumpet by the time they started kindergarten. They had the freedom to hang out at home and make their own fun.

If I may say so myself, my mooching philosophy sounded very impressive; well, it sounded better than admitting I just couldn't be stuffed getting me or the kids dressed to go anywhere.

Of course, there were some drawbacks to staying at home full-time. First and foremost was the fact that I lost touch with the real world. So much so that one day I walked into a local hairdresser's to get my shoulder-length hair trimmed only to emerge half an hour later with a full-on mullet. This would have been fine except they'd apparently stopped being fashionable some years earlier.

There were times while standing in the kitchen at number 26, still dressed in my pyjamas at two in the afternoon, stirring a pot of the aforementioned homemade playdough, that I would yearn for some contact with the outside world. Often I wanted more than contact; I wanted to be part of it. It was an especially exciting time in the Melbourne comedy scene with venues such as the Last Laugh and Comedy Café helping to launch the careers of Wendy Harmer, Jean Kittson and the young, unknown Judith Lucy. It felt like I was being left behind. Who was I kidding? I *was* being left behind. Meanwhile, John was working really long hours. This meant that I was often starved for adult company; at times I felt plain lonely. Sure, I experienced a strong bond with Greg Evans and Dexter and the *Perfect Match* couples but sometimes they just weren't enough.

That's why I was so excited the day my friend Lynda Gibson rang me and suggested we resurrect a comedy act we'd created years before while working in the clown ensemble in Albury. I jumped at the chance.

The new, revised edition of The Natural Normans consisted of me, Lynda, Lynne McGranger (famous for her role as Irene on *Home and Away*) and music theatre performer, Sally Anne Upton. We performed as a group of sleazy male singers who sang disgustingly sexist songs about women. What the Normans lacked in talent they made up for in ridiculously gigantic egos. We wore dinner suits with pink sequined lapels, lemon-coloured shirts and pencilled-on moustaches. We specialised in extremely cheesy choreography.

For our first performance we headed out of town, to a comedy night at a snow resort up at Falls Creek. It was a two-night booking – the first time I'd been away from the kids. I was ecstatic. We did our first night and it was fine; in fact, we were quietly confident that we might just have a raging success on our hands. And so we celebrated, a lot, and, in keeping with the spirit of all things snow-related, we got stuck into the apple schnapps. What a night. This was like a fairytale existence. I was away working, John was at home looking after the kids, and I had company, great company; no offence to Greg and Dexter but these girls really knew how to party. God, we laughed. We laughed and laughed and laughed until …

… the next morning. That's when Sal rocked up to the room that Lynda and I were sharing. Lynda was in the top bunk as my legs had proved too short to swing myself up there, especially after a night on the apple schnapps. I was in the bottom bunk.

'Gib, Scotty, wake up.'

'What's wrong, Sal?'

'Fucking hell, what a fucking morning. I woke up, took one look at Lynne and thought, "Jesus fucking Christ, she doesn't look too crash hot." So I tried to wake her and fuck me, she's unconscious, completely fucking unconscious. I had to call the doctor. Just as well they've got one here on the mountain. She's got alcoholic poisoning, specifically apple fucking schnapps poisoning. There's no fucking way she's going to be able to perform tonight.'

Lynda's head appeared, hanging upside down over the edge of her bunk, 'Well, what do you reckon we do, Scotty?'

'I don't know. What d'you reckon, Sal?'

'Fucked if I know, darl.'

We went to check on Lynne. It wasn't a pretty sight. How can a human being be that pale and wretched and bilious and still be alive? We reworked the act for three, rehearsing in the room where Lynne was in bed, so we could keep checking that she hadn't choked to death on her own vomit. But as the saying goes, 'There's no business like show business' and when the curtain went up that night there were four Normans on stage, one of us a distinct shade of green.

Dressing as a man and getting to swagger about on stage as an untalented, egotistical, sexist, sleazy, pelvic-thrusting guy was really quite an invigorating experience. So this is how it felt, hey, to have not much more going for you than a penis. We even had women in the audience hot for us, I mean screaming for us, wanting us and, more to the point, waiting for us after the show, baby. The fact that we were all utterly heterosexual seemed to make no difference, and in fact this only added to the general gender confusion after the shows. Lesbians would be shaking their heads, asking themselves, 'What the hell is going on here? I'm attracted to a Norman! Sure, he's really a woman, but I became sexually attracted when she was dressed as a he and behaving like a disgusting pig of a man.' Meanwhile groups of straight women would scream during the show as though they were at a Tom Jones gig and yes, the occasional pair of underpants was thrown! You'd see these same women at the bar afterwards, looking confused. Were the lesbians straight? Were the straight women lesbian? Whichever way you looked at it, the Natural Normans blew the ladies' minds. And we were successful. The Normans went on to perform in comedy venues and festivals throughout Australia. We were on a winner!

Of course, there was the occasional dud gig, such as the night we performed at a uni campus where the audience of a thousand male engineering students began chanting, 'FUCK OFF, FUCK OFF, FUCK OFF!' Amazingly, when we did eventually oblige them and dance off-stage, we turned around to see Lynne 'there's-no-business-like-show-business' McGranger had automatically danced right back on again to do an encore.

At the same time as the Normans were on their way to achieving Rolling Stones status, the theatre company John worked for folded so he was now freelancing, still doing gigs as a policewoman. This was a tremendous stroke of luck as it meant that John was now free to share parenting and housework duties. Hip, hip, hoorah! It was my dream come true: we could both work, both parent, and our kids could still mooch. Could life have been any more idyllic? In fact, if I'd had to witness the same good fortune being visited on another family I would have vomited with envy. John and I would give each other a high-five at the front door as he arrived home dressed as a woman and I headed off dressed as a man.

'So how would you girls like to perform in the Edinburgh Festival?' The Normans were gathered in our agent Nanette's office for a career meeting. Lynne screamed, 'Oh my Lordy, Nanette, are you serious? That's been my dream, hasn't it, girls, to perform at that festival!'

'Fuckin' brilliant,' Sal said enthusiastically.

Lynda was wary. 'It's a long way to go to get told to fuck off.'

'How much will it cost us?' Sal continued, keeping the ball rolling.

I remained silent.

Nanette sucked harder than ever on her cigarette and exhaled slowly as she did some mental calculations. 'Let's see. There's your return airfares, your accommodation for the month, publicity costs, posters, flyers, festival registration, venue hire, and then of course your daily expenses for food, drink, et cetera, which are exorbitant at the festival … I reckon you'd be looking at … um… oh … about six or seven grand.'

'Between us?'

'No, each.'

'Holy fucking shit!'

Nanette continued, 'Yes, Sal, it's a lot of money but if you do well, which, let's face it, you girls should, you'll make that money back in ticket sales and you could even make a profit. More to the point, this trip could really open some doors. I wouldn't be at all surprised if you got a follow-up season in London for a couple of weeks.'

A few days later the Normans were all in the kitchen at number 26. We were having an Edinburgh planning meeting. There was a lot of talk about accommodation, where we would perform, if we'd get any time to check out the sights.

'I can't go.'

The girls looked at me. 'What?'

'I can't go to Edinburgh. I've got the kids.'

'John can look after them.'

'No, I couldn't be away from them for six weeks.'

'Of course you could. I had a friend who went overseas and left her kids at home and she said once she was on the plane she forgot they'd ever existed.'

'Maybe John and the kids could come with you.'

I explained that this was impossible. We didn't have the money for my airfare let alone for the rest of the family. Sal was sympathetic, 'Well, darl, it's a fucking travesty but you've got to do what you've got to do.'

The Normans went to Edinburgh as a trio and I went back to Greg, Dexter and my pot of playdough.

CHAPTER 5

Birthday parties:
a cautionary tale

have a very good friend who set extremely high standards for kids' birthday parties but I've read a book by the Dalai Lama and he reckons I should let go of my resentment and forgive her. Which is easier said than done.

I first met Kirsty when she knocked on my door one day. She introduced herself and explained, 'I live around the corner and I have kids and I noticed you have a pusher sitting on your front porch and thought that you might have kids as well and if you do would you be interested in getting together sometime?'

Who would've thought there were pick-up lines for stay-at-home mothers? Anyway, it worked. Kirsty and I got together with our kids regularly and it was always fun.

Kirsty was one of those mums who would encourage her children to climb up onto the shed roof, drop raw eggs and watch them splatter on the concrete below, all in the name of understanding gravity. Being a mum seemed to come so easily and naturally to her that I'm pretty sure she gave birth to her third child during one of our playgroup sessions and none of us noticed.

Being invited to one of Kirsty's theme parties was like stepping inside an Enid Blyton novel. For starters, there was the masked fairy ball – thirty little kids between four and five years old all dressed as fairies. I spent a week making both my kids a set of papier-mâché fairy wings, hand-decorating them with sequins, baubles and lace. And to think I once turned up my nose at that mask-making workshop at teachers' college as having no relevance to my future life! I was surprised how easily it all came back to me; although asking your child to sit still while smearing their little face with Vaseline, then covering it in wet gypsona bandages and waiting until it sets into a plaster-cast can be quite tricky. My kids didn't say a word throughout the whole procedure; admittedly, they did try at one point but by then the plaster had set. Bonnie wore a pale-pink party frock she already had hanging in the wardrobe; but to be perfectly frank, my knowledge of what a young man wears to a fairy ball was limited. I ended up dressing Jordie in a neck-to-ankle, pale-blue lycra leotard that I had once worn in a creative movement performance at teachers' college. (Boy, that course really did come in handy.) Once the wings and a sequined belt were added to the costume, I felt quietly confident that I had the boy-fairy concept pretty well nailed. The notion of a goblin look, featuring some sort of green hat and a set of big plastic ears bought from a magic shop never occurred to me – until I arrived at the masked fairy ball to see that goblins were all the go for little boys. But hey, at the end of the day who won the Best Boy Dressed as a Fairy prize? As Kirsty explained to all the disappointed little goblins, the reason for her decision was that 'Jordie was the only boy at the party brave enough to wear fairy wings.' Oh yeah, we took home the prize booty that day. Not that I'm a competitive mother, just extremely caring.

Kirsty's creative party ideas didn't stop there; the family kept topping themselves, which was exactly what I felt like doing when my kids got invited to their grand prix party. Making masks was one thing but a homemade billy cart? We hadn't made those at teachers' college.

Then there was the rodeo party that featured a homemade bucking bronco made from a big hessian bag stuffed with straw, with ropes tied at both ends and slung between two trees like a hammock. A child would sit astride the bag while the birthday boy's father would feverishly yank the ropes up and down until the kid fell off onto the mattresses piled below. Yahoo, ride 'em cowboy!

But the real knockout A-list social event on any under ten's calendar was the year Kirsty's family held a medieval ball. It was going to be their biggest party ever as they'd announced they were heading overseas indefinitely, making this possibly their last themed party. Oh, thank Christ, I sighed.

But for now we were faced with the mother of all kids' parties and John and I responded with appropriate zeal and an almost obsessive, manic desire to really excel. As I've mentioned, it's not that we're competitive, we just want to do the very best by our kids and if this means they end up looking better than everybody else's kids then so be it.

I was responsible for creating a Maid Marian look for Bonnie. The hair was simple: thick strands of yellow wool braided into plaits and then attached to a turban, which – and this may be hard to believe but it's true – I had used as a hat for one of the puppets I'd made at teachers' college. As for Bonnie's Maid Marian frock: what a piece of extraordinary luck. I was walking down our main street and there it was, sitting in the window of our local antique shop. In fact, I gasped when I saw it; it was a deranged mother's dream come true: a pale-blue, full-length number featuring a satin bodice with silver trim and a mass of fluffy tulle under the chiffon skirt. I couldn't believe it. As a theatre director at teachers' college once said of a show we'd written ourselves: 'It's good but where's your wow factor?' As I stood there gaping at this dress I thought to myself, well, there's certainly no questioning the 'wow' factor in this situation. It was the perfect choice for a young girl wanting to make a dazzling, awe-inspiring entrance to a medieval ball. I could see it in my mind's eye: Maid

Marian galloping through Sherwood Forest, her woollen plaits flying out behind her. When she arrived at the castle and walked into the ball, all the guests, including Robin Hood and his band of merry men, would look at her and say as one: 'Wow!'

I went into the shop and asked the antique-seller, 'How much for the dress?'

'Sixty dollars,' he replied.

Phew, what fantastic news because would you believe it? We had $72 in the bank.

Meanwhile John had been holed up in the shed, consumed by all the manic artistic verve of a young, crazed Salvador Dali. It was his job to construct Jordie's dragon outfit. He spent days feverishly designing, cutting, sawing, drilling, painting, stapling and gluing until he finally emerged triumphant, holding aloft an enormous dragon's head. It was made out of cardboard and featured a huge open mouth with jagged teeth and orange and yellow cellophane flames spewing forth. It was designed to be worn over the top of Jordie's head and held in place by two ribbons tied in a big bow underneath the chin, Easter bonnet–style. But the *pièce de résistance* was the dragon's tail, approximately six metres long, made out of chicken wire stuffed with newspaper and covered in green stretch fabric.

The day of the medieval ball finally arrived. Bonnie was dressed and waiting in the car. Jordie was sitting next to her in his bottle-green skivvy, a pair of my green ribbed pantihose and his yellow gumboots. The rest of the dragon outfit was being carefully packed into the boot of the car. We headed off in the family Datsun, driving slowly and cautiously, aware of the precious cargo we had onboard (the dragon suit, not the kids). We parked the car just around the corner from the party venue. John carefully placed the dragon's head on top of Jordie's and tied it in place. I safety-pinned the tail to his bottom. John and I followed as Bonnie and Jordie slowly headed towards the party hand in hand (because Jordie couldn't see where he was going). Bonnie lifted the latch on the white-picket gate and that's when we heard the first guttural cry.

'Dragon! There's a dragon!'

It had simply never occurred to John and me that every other boy at the party would be dressed as a knight. More to the point, it appears that no matter what era you live in, or how old you are, when the male of the species sees a dragon he has to kill it. Parents came from everywhere and vainly tried to rescue Jordie. But when the bloodlust has been released and about thirty knights brandishing cardboard swords and yelling 'Kill, kill, kill!' make a charge at their victim, there is little that can be done to stop it. One lot tore off his head and ripped it to shreds while the others wrenched his tail from his bottom and jumped up and down on it until it was just a flattened, unrecognisable mess of paper and wire.

Some years later, when this theme-party family had returned to Australia, the eldest daughter had a combined fourteenth birthday party with her stepsister. These girls were stunningly beautiful, as were all of their friends. Jordie wasn't invited to the party; he was *paid* to attend. That's right, at twelve years of age Jordie was too young to be of interest as a guest but by this stage he had formed his first musical partnership with a kid called Simon and this party was their first paid gig. Simon and Jordie were both short and Jordie was a little tubster who wore his hair parted in the middle and kind of plastered to his head with some disgusting cheap, sick-smelling gel. But man, these guys could play their acoustic and electric guitars, they could sing in perfect harmony and they wrote their own fantastic songs. What I'm trying to say is that Jordie walked into that party a short, chubby, self-conscious little boy. An hour later he walked out a man.

Yeah ... I guess ... um ... yeah ... I guess what I'm trying to say is that just because, you know, when you're a kid you get the crap beaten out of you doesn't mean that for the rest of your life you are going to be that dragon. You know what I'm sayin'? I mean, like, having your friends rip your head off your shoulders and your tail off your arse kind of helps to make you a much more, you know, sort of psychologically damaged adult and that's great for ... you know ... writing songs. So yeah ... thanks a lot all you guys.

Jordie, on stage at the Brunswick Hotel, 2007.

CHAPTER 6
Cousin Gavin's underpants

t was a hot summer's night so our front and back doors were wide open, as were most of our windows. The family was eating dinner, our favourite: crumbed cutlets and mashed potatoes. Jordie began sniffing, 'Hey, I can smell something.'

We all paused from our cutlet experience.

'Yeah, you're right, Jords. There is something …'

'Smells a bit like smoke …'

'Yeah, I wonder where it's coming from?'

'Keith must be having a barbecue,' Jordie concluded, and we all resumed eating our cutlets.

I don't know how a family sitting in a house with all its doors and windows open could have missed four massive fire-trucks, sirens blaring, pull up and start hosing the next door neighbour's place. I don't know how a family, usually keen to experience anything that breaks the monotony of everyday life, could have missed the ambulance arriving, or all the neighbours racing to the scene, or the crackling of the flames that were licking so close to our own house, or the black billowing smoke, or even the initial God-almighty bang as the pot of boiling oil that Keith had left on his stove exploded in a ball of flames. All I can say is our crumbed cutlets must have been pretty darn good.

Keith had been our neighbour ever since we moved in to number 26. He'd been renting his old federation home for years. He was a man who wore a navy singlet and shorts all year round. He liked his beer and made his meagre income from delivering junk mail, which he wheeled along in an old pram; we never had the heart to put a No Junk Mail sticker on our letterbox. His heart was as big and warm as a brandy-soaked Christmas pudding and his face was as red as the glacé cherry that sits on top (even redder the night of the fire).

From the day we moved in, Keith took us under his wing, declaring that he'd do whatever he could to help us out. I'd arrive home to find sitting on our front verandah bits of furniture, including dining-room chairs, a phone table and even a clothes-horse, that Keith had found while out delivering pamphlets.

After the fire the land was sold to developers, but before the house was demolished Keith sneaked onto the property late one night, 'stole' the federation verandah posts which had survived the flames and gave them to us as a parting gift, 'Just in case youse ever decide to renovate.'

Keith was far from the only person to give us second-hand goods. John and I seemed to give off a vibe that said, 'If you don't want it, we'll take it.' What am I talking about? There was no vibe involved; John actually said these words, often to total strangers. Pretty soon it was commonplace for relatives and friends, and friends of friends, and friends of friends of friends, to ring us and say, 'Yeah, hi there. Look, you haven't met me but I got your number from your friend Paul, who I met at a party and he said you might be interested in this old kitchen cupboard that I'm getting rid of. Are you? Because if you don't take it, it's going to go to the tip.'

We were the equivalent of the lost dogs' home for furniture. We were, or more specifically John was (and still is), suckers for saving unwanted, unloved and, for that matter, often unusable wardrobes, chairs and beds from ending their days being mulched to pieces under a mountain of clay.

It was thanks to this principle that my cousin Gavin's underpants came to reside at our house. Not that they were old. They were pretty close to being new, which is why my Aunty Noreen brought them to my mother's house and left them there for John to pick up when he was next visiting. We also inherited Gavin's ugg boots. Now let me quickly make it clear that Gavin had not met an untimely death. Goodness me, no; he had simply moved out of home to go and live in Darwin. I guess that explains why he no longer needed his ugg boots. But hang on, what's a sheep if not just a giant ugg boot on four legs? And there are plenty of sheep happily living up north, so ... oh bloody hell, so many questions, so few answers. All I know for sure is that we inherited them.

Initially John tried to claim ownership. 'But Scotty, your Aunty Noreen said they were for me.'

'Yes, John, but Gavin is my cousin.'

And so the ugg boots became 'our' slippers, and whoever got up first got to wear them. In fact, they became the family's communal slippers as Jordie and Bonnie also became keen on using Uncle Gavin's ugg boots to slide around the house.

As for cousin Gavin's underpants, and his reason for not wanting to take them to Darwin: I can only conclude that it was Darwin's stifling heat and humidity because God knows what a pair of bri-nylon jocks could do to a man in those circumstances. Thus, these pale-brown with dark-brown trim, 100 per cent synthetic underpants in as-good-as-new condition went in the drawer and became John's emergency pair. If only they'd stayed in that drawer I would never have had to endure one of the most humiliating experiences of my life, an experience that gave a whole new meaning to the phrase, 'Always leave the house wearing good underpants. You never know when you may have sex in a highly public place.'

It was maybe a couple of years after the arrival of the second-hand underpants that I flew to Sydney where I had two weeks' work acting in a telemovie for SBS. It was called *Piccolo Mondo*, written by Andrew Bovell and directed by Sue Brooks. During the second week's filming, John and the kids flew to Sydney and stayed with me. Their arrival was to have an unforeseen consequence that to this day makes me shudder.

Filming was an all-round brilliantly satisfying experience but towards the end of the shoot came the day I was dreading: the day I had to record my first, and consequently only, sex scene. Oh, even now my stomach churns at the thought. In the film, my character Katherine was a plain, lonely, single nurse who, while she was out having lunch with her two girlfriends at an upmarket restaurant, fantasised about having sex with the young Italian waiter. It was this wild fantasy that was to be filmed. The afternoon before filming the scene, I psychologically prepared by going for a full-leg and bikini wax.

The next morning I tried to appear nonchalant and unfazed. I sauntered onto the set wearing my nurse's uniform where Angelo d'Angelo, the actor playing the waiter, was already waiting for me. 'Hi Angelo,' I said in a way-too-loud, weird sort of voice. He was the most gorgeous-looking man with an exquisite body, perfect olive skin, stunning dark-brown eyes, beautiful curly hair, and a smile that made you swoon. Good God, was I falling in love? Quite possibly – I'd read somewhere that an actress, maybe Julia Roberts or Meg Ryan, said that for the duration of a film she always fell in love with her leading man; it helped her acting.

And so, while I desperately concentrated on falling in love with Angelo, at least to the point where I could have sex with him in public, Sue called for a closed set. A closed set! Why? A closed set is when all crew who aren't absolutely essential to that particular scene must leave the studio. This was to give Angelo and me some privacy. Privacy? What the hell did Sue think was going to happen? I started to wonder about things, like would our bottoms actually have to touch? Oh God, I was going to be sick. What a relief it was to hear Sue inform us that Angelo, who was wearing a crisp white shirt, would be able to wear a g-string, and she was pretty sure I'd be able to keep my underpants on as she didn't think they would be seen. Hooray! No chance of a Sharon Stone *Basic Instinct* mishap when a girl's got her underpants safely and securely in place.

Angelo d'Angelo and I took up our starting positions. I was standing with my back against the wall in the restaurant. My nurse's shoes and pantihose were on the floor beside me, my dress pulled up around my hips. Angelo stood facing me, wearing his shirt and g-string. His pants were down around his ankles. Sue called, 'Action.' Away Angelo and I went. What can I say? We let all our inhibitions go and lost ourselves in a lovemaking frenzy, the likes of which hadn't been seen on the screen since the famous butter incident with Marlon Brando and

Maria Schneider in *Last Tango in Paris*. Suddenly Sue called, 'Cut.'

She walked over to Angelo and me, looking very serious. 'What you two are doing is fantastic, absolutely perfect, but …' and she turned towards me, 'I'm sorry, Scotty, the underpants have to go. We can see them.'

If I thought doing a sex scene in public was humiliating, what happened next can only be described as excruciating torture, for it was then that I realised I was wearing cousin Gavin's bri-nylon underpants because I'd run out and John had brought them with him to Sydney. This would have been fine except that, for camera reasons, I had to remain on set while I removed them, in front of everyone. Then it was the wardrobe lady's job to walk onto the set and take them from me. The point is, the studio was hot. I was hot. I was hot and I was sweaty with nerves. The underpants were bri-nylon. Am I making myself clear? Remember why Gavin didn't take the underpants to Darwin? High temperatures and bri-nylon do not a good marriage make, that's all I'm trying to say. My memory is of the wardrobe lady, looking as though she was about to dry-retch, gingerly taking my cousin Gavin's underpants from me and holding them at some distance as she carried them off-set, where she was charged with keeping them on 'stand-by' in case we reached a point where I could put them on again.

A few days after I'd finished the film shoot and returned to Melbourne, I answered the door to find

Geoff, another neighbour with a fondness for beer, standing there with a garbage bag in his hand. 'G'day Denise. I was given this bag of stuff just before and thought you could probably use it.'

I opened the bag. It was day-old bread from the local bakery. 'But Geoff, haven't you heard? I'm a movie star now.' Well, that's what I *wanted* to say but I just sighed and quietly slumped in that 'I've just done a sex scene in my cousin Gav's synthetic underpants and been given a bag of day-old bread by a young, well-meaning unemployed alcoholic' sort of way. 'Thanks Geoff,' I said, resisting the temptation to add, 'I'll make the kids some bread and dripping for dinner.'

CHAPTER 7

A new bed and a shocking nightmare

ne day, admittedly without warning, I suggested to John that we get a new bed. He looked at me as though I'd just announced I'd grown a penis. 'But Scotty, I love our bed.'

'So do I, John, but the base is broken …'

'I told you I was going to fix it, Scotty.'

'John, that was six years ago. And the futon – the mould's getting worse; I reckon that's why we're all coughing.'

'Our coughing's not that bad.'

'John, we sound as if we're in a 1930s tuberculosis ward … or whenever it was that people had tuberculosis.'

'I know, Scotty, but I do just love our bed.'

The truth was we all loved that disgusting bed. It was our haven, a refuge from the outside world. Tuberculosis was a small price to pay for the joy and love we felt when we were all snuggled up in it together. The kids had slept with us the first few years of their lives; it simply made sense to John and me to have the kids in bed with us and it made breastfeeding a breeze. I breastfed Bonnie until she was two and it meant she could just help herself; I didn't even have to really be awake. Of course, this meant that sometimes I'd wake up with one breast its normal bowling-ball size while the other would be the size of a pickled walnut.

When the kids were a bit older and had their own beds, we'd still gather round and eat breakfast on the futon. John would bring us croissants fresh from the local bakery, smothered in melting butter and strawberry jam. The kids would have apple juice and John and I would have a steaming cup of strong coffee made in the espresso pot. Sometimes John would make pancakes dripping with maple syrup. Consequently, by the end of its life our futon was not only covered in mould, but also breastmilk, blood, children's urine, spilt coffee, maple syrup, massage oil, herbal eczema potions and vomit stains which, to be honest, didn't bother me because hey, apart from us, who was ever going to see them?

All our neighbours and the many pedestrians who passed by our house the day John decided to air our futon in our little front yard, that's who. I'd been at work. I couldn't believe my own horrified eyes when I arrived home to see that mattress hanging over a clothes–horse in our front yard, so brutally displaying the detailed and intimate history of every single orifice of every single member of our family.

At that very moment our tiny, elderly neighbours, Giovanni and Sebastiana, walked passed and stopped to have a good look. They seemed puzzled. 'Hey Denise, what's this?' Giovanni gestured towards the futon.

I gulped. If you could die of embarrassment I surely would've dropped dead. 'Oh that. Um … that's something … um … we … John … um … he … found it in the garage. Must have belonged to the people who used to live here before us.' Giovanni just stood there looking amused, shaking his head and his hands in that classic old–style Italian, I–don't–get–these–crazy–Australians sort of way. Sebastiana, who didn't speak English, simply looked mystified. I walked in the front door.

'Jesus Christ, John, have you no shame?'

'What are you talking about, Scotty?'

'The futon.'

'What about the futon?'

'It's in the front garden.'

'I know. I'm airing it.'

'Everyone can see it.'

'So?'

'It looks disgusting.'

'It's not that bad.'

'Not that bad? If human services walked past they'd take the kids off us.'

'Scotty, it's a symbol of our life, that's all.'

It was then John agreed we would get a new bed – a real bed with a fat mattress with miracoil inner springs, and a real bed-base with bed-ends. For its final public journey from our house to the tip in the back of a friend's ute, I covered both sides of the futon with a couple of king-size sheets. Even mattresses deserve to die with dignity.

We purchased a king-size colonial reproduction cheap pine situation with tulips cut out of the slats at both bed-ends. As the young salesman said at the time, 'The tulips, aren't they lovely?'

'Yes,' I replied, 'But I do find it a bit odd ...'

'What do you find odd?'

'Well, I find it hard to imagine that some convict living in an old tent on the dusty rough-as-guts goldfields would have had the time or, for that matter the inclination, to carve tulip shapes out of his bed-head.'

The salesman looked at me like I was an unfathomable idiot and John, always one to enjoy a historical discussion, suggested, 'It would've been more likely your government officials who chose the tulip design.'

'Oh, whatever ...' I was getting tense. I wasn't used to buying new things.

We didn't actually purchase the bed that day. We had to order one to be made especially for us because even though every single one of the hundred furniture stores we visited sold the exact same bed, NO ONE in the history of modern-day pine furniture had ever wanted a

KING–SIZE colonial reproduction cheap pine situation with tulips cut out of the slats at both bed–ends.

I realised why on the day the bed was delivered. What had looked quite reasonable displayed in a huge showroom suddenly looked extraordinarily, massively, ridiculously huge when the king–size version was set up in our relatively small bedroom. With its height and the bed–ends, it seemed much more imposing than our low-lying futon. As I often do at times of self–imposed disappointment, I burst into sobs and wailed inconsolably, 'I hate it! It looks ugly, really ugly …'

'Scotty, it looks lovely.'

'It doesn't, John, it looks hideous. Oh, what's wrong with us? Other people choose nice things. We pick shit.'

'Scotty, we chose each other.'

I paused and decided to ignore his comment because it was only going to distract me from proceeding ever onwards to a full–blown hysterical tantrum.

'John, look at the size of the bed, and look at those tulips; they're revolting.'

'Scotty, you love tulips.'

'I love tulips when they're in a vase, John, or in a field in Holland with a windmill and fair–haired rosy–cheeked boys and girls in clogs. I don't love them when they're carved into a cheap pine bed that happens to be the size of Tasmania.'

'Scotty, the bed is exactly the same size as the futon; it just *seems* bigger.'

'So, you agree it's ridiculous?'

'No, I agree that it appears to be bigger but the reality is it isn't; and besides Scotty, you loved this bed when we first saw it. You said, "John, look at this bed. Isn't it gorgeous?"'

'Yes, I did think that, John, and I thought the same thing when I first saw a cane toad ...'

'What are you talking about now?'

'When I first saw a cane toad I thought, "Gee, isn't that cute?" The same with rabbits, maybe even mice, but by the time you've seen them everywhere and realise that they are an out-of-control plague, you think they are ugly, right? So that's what I felt by the time I saw this tulip bed in the hundredth store. In fact, do you want to know what I really thought?'

'What?'

'I thought, "Jeez, Ned Kelly was better off swinging from a noose. At least that way he'd never have to look at another colonial tulip bed again."'

'If you didn't like the bed, why did you agree to buy it?'

'The same reason we bought the house: ugly but cheap! John, seriously, tell me the truth, did the bed look this awful when we saw it in the shop?'

'No, no, it didn't.'

'Oh no ...'

'What?'

'So you agree that it looks awful, and when you say something looks awful, John, then that means it's got to be really, seriously awful,' I sobbed.

'Scotty, I don't think it's awful; in fact, I reckon it's going to be great.'

'Going to be great? What do you mean, *going* to be great? How is it *going* to be great? You think it's *going* to grow up and blossom like an ugly ducking into a beautiful swan? It's a bed, John. It's at the end of its journey. It's a fait accompli.'

'I reckon we get a new doona and some pillows; you know, those big fat oversized European ones, and they'll make a big difference. Our little flat pillows are not in proportion with the bed.'

John and I then lay down on the bed. It has to be said that my tears quickly subsided as our bodies experienced the bliss of the new and wondrous mattress. John, who's always been a very vocal chap, let out a variety of moaning sounds indicating his deep, deep, deep pleasure … until he rolled over to face me.

'Oh no, I don't believe this.'

'What?'

'The bed-base. It's bending.'

The wooden slat bed-base had bent in the middle as though we were in a hammock. And this, it has to be said, was in the days when we were slim. John began to roll over onto his back again. The bed *boi-oi-oi-oing*ed and bowed even more.

'John, stop … the bed-base, it's going to snap in half.'

John and I lay there frozen stiff, both of us holding our breath, too scared to move. Slowly and surely John began to inch his way off the bed. I then followed suit. Carefully, we dragged off our new fat mattress and studied the wooden slats. They were too thin and the sheer width of the king-size bed – which the man at the factory had never made before – meant that they couldn't cope with any weight on them at all. John, being experienced in this particular dilemma, headed off to the garage and returned with a couple of milk crates that he put under the middle of the bed. He then put a six-foot-six length of thick scaffolding wood on top of the milk crates which was used to balance the base of the bed.

'We'll have to ring the bed people in the morning and get it sorted out.'

A couple of weeks later, the phone rang at 3 am. I woke in fright. Ever since that early call from Mum telling me that Dad was 'in a bad way', I had come to associate middle-of-the-night calls with bad, very bad, news. I flew into the hallway, my stomach lurching, my whole body bracing itself for a shock. I picked up the phone.

'Hello?'

'Hello Scotty, it's Sophia.'

Even that simple piece of news was enough to shock me. I had expected a relative, not a mum from the kids' school.

'Sophia, what is it? Is everything alright?'

'It's your children …'

A chill of truly Alfred Hitchcock proportions penetrated the very core of my being. 'What about my children?'

'They're here.'

'What?'

'Your children, they're at my house.'

At this point I did a quick round-up of all the mad, panicked thoughts that were racing around inside my head and came to the conclusion that Sophia must have been having a complete nervous breakdown. I calmed myself and said, 'Sophia, my kids are in bed asleep.'

'Scotty, they're at my house.'

'Sophia, hang on a minute.'

I ran into the kids' room and turned on the light. Both beds were empty. I felt sick. I couldn't fathom what was going on. Mad, panicked thoughts once again took off inside my head. I began embellishing the nervous breakdown theory, so by the time I was back at the phone I'd concluded that Sophia had somehow kidnapped my children. At this point let me stress that Sophia was a wonderful friend whose major characteristic was a passion for people and life which sometimes led to an exciting, dramatic social event, but this hardly made her a child abductor. Yet the time for rational thinking had long passed. 'Sophia, we're on our way,' I said.

I ran into the bedroom where John, who is a good sleeper, was still dozing. I was crazed. 'John, the kids …'

John sat bolt upright.

'... they're at Sophia's.'

'What? Why, why, what do you mean they're at Sophia's?'

Good question. What would a five-year-old and a three-year-old be doing at three o'clock in the morning at a friend's house at least four blocks away?

John wasted no time in pulling on an overcoat and grabbing his car keys. On our way to Sophia's, it was dark, it was foggy, it was eerily quiet. I almost expected to hear the distant sound of horses' hooves clippity-clopping along the cobblestone road, coming closer and closer until a horse and carriage appeared in full view, driven by an evil-looking chap with a big black cape and a weird glint in his glass eye – replacing the eye he'd lost in a recent swashbuckling episode at a nearby inn. And as the carriage raced past us I would gasp because ... oh, what was that? Could it be? Oh my God, no! Little Bonnie and Jordie's frightened faces peering out of the carriage window ...

We pulled up at Sophia's. She opened the front door. She was wearing her reassuring fluffy pink dressing gown and smoking a reassuring cigarette and drinking a reassuring cup of instant coffee. Bonnie, who was wearing her new polka-dot pyjamas, raced out into the hallway looking excited, quite thrilled in fact. Her big eyes were way bigger than normal. 'Hi Mum,' she said, giving me a hug.

Sophia led us into the lounge where Jordie was sitting in a large leather lounge chair. He had on his little navy dressing gown that looked so warm and cosy but as was the case with most cheap clothing for kids, was in fact fully synthetic and sported a label advising you to keep well away from heaters as it was highly flammable. Jordie had his head down, his hands clasped anxiously in his lap. John and I tried to be nonchalant. 'Hi Jordie.'

'Hi ...' he whispered. He seemed on the verge of tears. He couldn't speak.

Sophia explained that she had been woken by a knock at her door at around 2.45 am. She had freaked out and assumed the worst, and had headed off to find a piece of four-by-four with which to hit the assailants on the head. Thus, by the time she finally got to the front door, there was no one there. Then she gingerly walked out into the street, brandishing the big piece of wood, ready to strike, and that's when she saw two little kids in their dressing gowns running down the road. She caught up with them and brought them back to her place.

Jordie explained to her that he'd been dreaming there were robbers in our house. He woke up in fright and came running into our room, but we weren't in our bed – or so he thought. Because of the new bed, with a bed-end and our new big, fat, puffy doona, he hadn't been able to see us. It was at this point that Jordie, at five years of age, came to the irrefutable conclusion that his parents had been dragged into the backyard and murdered, and it was now his job to save his sister.

Apparently, Jordie then tiptoed back to the bedroom and woke Bonnie, whispering the news that her parents had been slaughtered and that they now had to escape or would be killed too. In absolute silence they set about putting on their dressing gowns. Jordie pulled on his yellow gumboots and then helped Bonnie put on her little navy lace-up shoes, including tying a double knot. (As a parent I found it really impressive that even in an extreme emergency, such as your parents being garrotted in the backyard, these children had remained so level-headed and practical.)

They then sneaked out the front door and ran like the blazes into the dark and misty night. It's difficult to run in gumboots but courage goes a long way to overcoming obstacles. All Jordie knew was that by now the robbers would most likely be looking for him and Bonnie. He knew he had to save his little sister, no matter what.

Meanwhile, Bonnie was having the time of her life, her only problem being that the legs of her pyjama pants were about a foot too long and she kept tripping over them. They ran across the street and through a big empty carpark, they crossed another street and then went through a small park with enormous palm trees looming scarily overhead. When a car drove down the street they quickly hid behind a bush. Finally, they made it to Sophia's house, which, naturally enough, was cloaked in darkness. Jordie's little fist knocked on Sophia's large glass-panelled door.

But seeing Sophia's dark silhouette holding aloft a huge piece of wood, once more they took off in fright. Sophia had run after them and brought them into the safety of her warm and homely lounge room, only to be told that we were lying dead in a pool of blood in our backyard.

In all the commotion, Sophia's kids had also woken up; so there we all were in our pyjamas, listening to Sophia's gripping account of the story. Throughout it all, Jordie sat in silence.

The next morning Jordie wouldn't go to school. He said all the other kids would have heard what had happened and he'd be laughed at. John and I assured him that he was mistaken. With absolute conviction we explained that he would be applauded for his courage. I proudly told him that if ever we *were* murdered, it was wonderful to know that he would save his sister. And so we made Jordie go to school.

Jordie was right. We were wrong. He was laughed at.

Seventeen years later we are still sleeping on that bed, which is still lying on top of scaffolding plank, which is still balancing on two milk crates.

CHAPTER 8
Head on

ne of the great features of number 26 is its location; it's a dream. It's in an ugly street with no trees, lots of rubbish and non-stop traffic BUT it is a one-minute walk from shops, trams and buses, and five minutes from a train. It is without doubt my nirvana, it's where I belong, it's my Dreaming, my true home. The reason it is so ideal is that unlike 99.9999 per cent of the Australian population, I don't drive. I used to but one day I stopped. Suddenly.

At twenty-three years of age I had a head-on car accident. I had just moved back to Melbourne, after having spent a year living in the wheat-farming town of Wycheproof. I hadn't gone there by choice; the government had sent me. I remember getting the letter informing me of the school I'd been posted to. I was at my mum and dad's place. I'd just finished my four years' training to be a secondary school teacher, majoring in drama and English. As I'd wanted to continue acting, I had applied to teach in all the groovy inner-suburban schools like Fitzroy, Collingwood and Richmond. Standing in the kitchen with my parents, I picked up the official letter. I opened it. I read it. I screamed.

'Wycheproof! Where the hell is Wycheproof?'

Luckily, Wycheproof had made it into Dad's RACV Victorian tourist guide. It was there because it has the smallest registered mountain in the world and because it has a train-line running down the middle of its main street.

I arrived with one suitcase and a small cardboard box of books, and moved into an old farmhouse that was twelve kilometres out of town, in a place called Teddy Waddy West.

Was I insane? Had I forgotten that I didn't drive? No, I had my pushbike. The idea of riding twenty-four kilometres a day really appealed to me. The Sunday evening before the school year was due to start, there was a getting-to-know-you barbecue where I met the other teachers and some of the parents. When I told them of my plan to ride my pushbike to school, they roared with laughter and mentioned things like wild bush pigs that had been known to kill. 'Humans?' I wanted to ask but felt a little foolish. They also mentioned something about headwinds but meteorology interested me about as much as the annual report from my superannuation fund, so I didn't listen and went to get another sausage instead.

The next morning I set off early on my ten-speed bike. It was glorious. The sun was shining golden on the wheat fields. The huge expanse of sky was a vivid, storybook blue. When I wasn't preoccupied with looking out for bush pigs, I marvelled at the pale and subtle silver of the giant gum trees. The road was straight and flat. I sailed along with a tailwind behind me. I'd left the city behind and I was happy. Man, I was euphoric! Utes were passing me full of kids being driven to school; they all tooted and waved. I would've waved back but I'd only recently taught myself to ride a two-wheeler so I couldn't let go of the handlebars. I arrived at the school early. It had only taken me twenty minutes or less. This was fantastic! I couldn't believe the locals weren't all into riding their bikes. Maybe I could educate them. But all that day, whenever I enthused about the joys of pushbike-riding to a local teacher or student, they'd just give me a knowing look and say something like, 'But you haven't ridden home yet.'

The afternoon was hot, really hot, typical of the intense heat the Mallee cooks up most summer days. I got on my bike and started pedalling. Within a minute I understood exactly what a headwind was — it was hot and it was strong and it was hell. I had my pride to think of so I changed gears, put my head down and pedalled. Man, did I pedal. My face was beetroot. I didn't look up. I just pedalled. I had to keep going.

After what seemed like an hour, a large Ford Fairlane pulled over in front of me. A mum called Diane and her daughter Cynthia, who was in my Year 7 English class, got out of their car. 'Would you like a lift?' I looked up at them all ready to say, 'No thanks, I'm fine,' but that's when I realised I was so parched that my tongue had stuck to the roof of my mouth and I couldn't speak. I also realised, to my utter dismay, that I was in exactly the same spot as when I'd started.

Diane got me some water from a nearby tank. She and her daughter hoisted me onto the back seat of their car, popped my bike in the boot, and took me home to their farmhouse where I was treated for dehydration and exhaustion. That's when I knew I was going to have to get my licence.

Gary was also a first-year-out English teacher. He taught me to drive in the hours and hours of downtime we had after school and on weekends. He had a mustard-coloured Renault and he was a good driving instructor, considering who he had to work with. I booked in to go for my licence one Friday afternoon. Gary wished me luck as I took off in the driver's seat of his Renault, the local policeman beside me in the passenger seat.

We went around the block. Then we headed up the road towards Mount Wycheproof, where there was an ever so slight incline. The policeman got me to brake, pause and then resume driving. Oh dear. We rolled backwards down that tiny little hill as I crunched and cranked my way through Gary's gears. Finally, I released the handbrake and that seemed to make a difference, so we putted up the mountain, did a U-turn and headed back towards town, where I was asked to pull up outside the grocer's. The policeman got out of the car, went into the store and emerged a minute later with the grocer and a customer. Under instruction from the policeman, they both got into their cars and proceeded to repark them in such a way that I could execute a reverse parallel park in between them. By now the word was out and a small crowd of locals had gathered to watch me park the car. Miraculously, I did it and they clapped. I got my licence and bought myself a white Mazda 808.

At the end of the year I decided to leave Wycheproof and move back to the city. It was a mistake. I hated teaching in the city.

On the evening that was to be the last time I would ever drive a car, I had been at a modern ballet class in Carlton. During the session the teacher asked us to come forward, one at a time, and stand in front of the huge floor-to-ceiling mirror that covered the entire wall. We then had to do a forward bend and check that our backs were straight. It came to my turn. I did my forward bend and was looking at my reflection when there was a sudden crack – not in my back, in the mirror. Pretty soon that one crack had spread its tentacles, and within seconds the whole mirror had shattered like a car windscreen that had been hit by a rock. My reflection was now broken into at least a thousand pieces. 'Jeez,' I thought, 'if breaking a little hand mirror means seven years' bad luck, what does a whole wall mean?' I was soon to find out.

I left the dance class, feeling decidedly spooked, unconvinced by the dance teacher's theory that the mirror had shattered because the woodfire heater nearby must have overheated the glass. I got into my white Mazda and headed off to a friend's place for dinner. I was travelling along Heidelberg Road on the inside lane when for some inexplicable reason I veered across to my right and went straight into oncoming traffic. Less than one minute later, I was able to step out of the wreck that seconds before had been my fully functional car. I knew with certainty that I'd hit something but I couldn't see another car anywhere. I thought, 'Wow, I must have hit a wall and I'm alive.' My spirits soared and I was about to thank God, when I turned around and saw it, the other vehicle, the one that had been innocently heading towards town.

The car was red. It was upside down. I saw bodies inside that car. I made a decision there and then. If I had killed someone, I was going to kill myself. It was a clear and irreversible plan. I stood alone, watching people running back and forth, trying to help the people trapped in the car. Tow-trucks arrived and the drivers circled around like desperate vultures, all thrusting their business cards at me. Fire-trucks were frantically unreeling their hoses and drenching the red car, telling onlookers to

'Move back, it could go up any second!' And here's when the miracle occurred. A young woman emerged from the wreckage. She was fine. She had been the sole occupant at the time of the crash.

Since I hadn't died in the accident, and didn't have to kill myself either, I rejoiced and felt that I'd been given a second crack at life. To celebrate, and as a way of offering thanks to the universe, I made two non-negotiable decisions. Firstly, I decided never to drive again. Secondly, I vividly remembered that at the point of impact – and this is absolutely the honest truth – I had what I thought was going to be my last ever thought: 'Oh Christ, I'm going to die, and I'm going to die a fucking teacher.'

The next day I quit.

CHAPTER 9

The war begins

alking out on stage to do a stand-up routine and having some guy in the audience yell out, 'Suck my cock, you fucking ugly mole!' before you've managed to say a single word does make one question one's career choice. And having your dignity shredded as easily as processed cheese in a metal grater does nothing for your general sense of wellbeing. So why did I decide to pursue stand-up comedy? Mental illness is one explanation that immediately springs to mind but the truth is, before I actually did it, I believed I'd be able to do a gig for twenty minutes, get paid okay money, then come straight home, get into bed, sleep soundly, rise the next morning all bright-eyed and bushy-tailed, look after the kids and run the house just as I'd always done. But wait, there's more! I honestly believed

that being a stand-up comedian would not only allow me to work as well as look after the kids and the house full-time but I could also achieve international stardom, go on to appear regularly on *The Dave Letterman Show,* be one of Michael Parkinson's favourite guests, and take over from the likes of Billy Crystal and Whoopi Goldberg to host the Academy Awards – all of which confirms my initial explanation – that I chose to do stand-up because I was at least a little bit mentally unwell.

The first cracks, or maybe fissures is a more apt description, in my flawed thinking began to appear the split-second I hung up the phone after having booked myself a 'try out' spot at a local comedy night. Immediately I felt sick with an anxiety the likes of which I'd never experienced before. I rang John, who was busy rehearsing a 'Galah Band' street act for the Royal Show.

'John …'

'Scotty, what's wrong?'

'I feel sick. My guts are churning.'

'What's happened?'

'I've just gone and booked myself in for a "try out" gig.'

'Scotty, that's great.'

'No, it's not. It's stupid, John. How the hell am I ever going to be able to write a stand-up comedy routine? I've got the kids. I've got to shop. I've got to cook. I've got to clean. I've got to visit Mum. I've got to take Bonnie to playgroup, Jordie to kinder. In fact, I've got to do milk and fruit at the kinder tomorrow. I've got to pay the bills. I've got to garden –'

'But Scotty, there is no garden; it's all concrete.'

'Don't be a smartarse, John, not now, this is serious. I've got to make fairy wings for Kirsty's fairy ball …'

'Why don't you just go and buy some?'

'Because, John, that would be a totally unfulfilling experience and they'd be crap whereas the kids and I could create a work of art together and get a lot of reward out of it.'

'Sure, but if it's going to cause you to have a nervous breakdown …'

'I'm not having a nervous breakdown about fairy wings, John; I'm having a nervous breakdown about doing stand-up comedy and getting everything done.'

'I'll help.'

'How?'

'I'll be home by six tonight and I'll do dinner.'

At seven o'clock that night the phone rang. 'I'm sorry, Scotty …'

'So am I, John. Where are you?'

'Still rehearsing. We've had problems with the galah dance on stilts but I think we've just about got it sorted.'

'Well, good for you.'

'I'll get us some takeaway on the way home.'

'Don't worry; we've eaten the leftover stew.' I sighed. Deeply.

'Scotty, what's the matter?'

'What do you mean, "what's the matter"? You're late.'

'I can't help it, I'm at work.'

'Well, what about me? Believe it or not, I've got work to do too but I can't because you're not here. But hey, as long as your galah family is happy …'

I told myself it was hopeless. Then I told myself it wasn't; after all, doesn't the best art come from human struggle? Yes, but usually the struggle is a more impressive one, such as surviving a concentration camp or swimming the English Channel with no arms. I started to sink again so this time I told myself that I had to keep calm and, more to the point, I had to keep moving forward. This meant getting the kids into bed and after they were settled I would start writing. This was a good plan.

I read the kids a bedtime story. Then I read them another one and another one. What the hell was in that leftover stew? Speed? The kids were still wide awake after ten o'clock when John finally arrived home. He'd had his hair cut to give the impression of a galah – shaved on the sides with a cockie's crest on top and streaked with bright-pink highlights. I said something appropriately cold and bitter to him before we agreed that he would try to settle the kids while I got stuck into my writing.

I sat down at the kitchen table, moved aside the plates and casserole pot, and placed a virgin notepad in front of me. I picked up a biro and held it poised above the piece of blank paper. I sat there. There wasn't a thought. Not a single thought. Oh God, come on brain, it's ten-thirty at night, I've got to do milk and fruit in the morning, I haven't got time not to have any thoughts. Please, please, please, God, please help me have a thought. By this stage, it wasn't just my mind but my entire body that was tense and straining with the sheer effort of producing a thought. I felt like a kid with constipation who still goes to the toilet and tries really hard anyway. Oh Jesus, this was torture. Nothing. I mean big, fat nothing. One big, fat nothing moment turned into two big, fat nothing hours.

I got up to make myself a cup of tea. I trod on some of the kids' Lego which was scattered all over the kitchen floor. 'Fuckitty fucking fuck, stupid, stupid, shitty little Lego … fucking fuck you.' I burst into tears.

John emerged from the kids' bedroom where he'd fallen asleep. His hairdo disturbed me.

'Scotty, how did your writing go?'

'How do you think it went, John? It's hopeless. I can't do this.'

'I think you can.'

'No, I can't.'

'Yes, you can.'

Had these been happier times, we would most likely have continued our banter until we both naturally burst into singing, 'I can do anything better than better, I can do anything better than you, no you can't, yes I can, no you can't, yes I can, yes I can, yes I can.' And we would have been singing our lungs out and laughing till we cried. But this was not a happy time.

'Scotty, you could be a great stand-up comic. You're talented, funny and clever.'

'Yeah sure, John, whatever. But you know what you really need to be a good stand-up comic?'

'What?'

'Time. Time to write a routine and I haven't got any time because you hog all the available time for your work.'

The war had begun.

Within a couple of months of doing stand-up, I decided that even if I couldn't have time I could at least have somewhere to go and sit and focus on my work. This was not hard to achieve: since the kids shared a bedroom, we had a spare room. In the corner of the room I set up a chair and a desk that we'd acquired from someone or other. So far, so good. I imagined that I would paint the room a calming shade of white, rip up the disgusting carpet and polish the floorboards. Maybe I would even purchase a small leather chesterfield couch and a Turkish carpet, and of course I would always have a clean glass vase full of fat blooming tulips. Needless to say, this was all a fantasy but what I really wanted more than anything in the world was for this room to be mine. I mean *all mine*.

'Scotty, are you saying you want the whole room just for you? I couldn't even have a small little corner of it?'

'That's exactly what I'm saying.'

'You wouldn't even let me have a small set of shelves in here?'

'No.'

'But that's not fair.'

'Too bad. I can't work with all your crap in here.'

'Well, where else can I put it?'

'John, you've got the shed.'

'But Scotty, it's full of wood that I'm saving in case we renovate one day.'

'I don't care, John. I can't think with all this stuff of yours around me.'

'Oh, I see. Just because a pair of my stilts is in the same room as you, you can't write a joke?'

'Oh, come on, John. It's not just a pair of stilts, it's all the funny hats and the old shoes and the suitcases full of stuff and the bags of juggling balls and the fire-twirling sticks and the costumes and the wigs and the lanterns and the huge pieces of foam and your personal collection of drums and ukuleles and maracas and castanets and all those old pots and pans which hey, I know are crucial to the creation of a percussive primitive beat in a street parade but Jesus, John, I'm telling you they're psychologically bringing me down.'

'So what you're saying is that basically all the difficulties you're having doing stand-up are my fault.'

'Yep, pretty much that is what I'm saying.'

'Well, that's just not true, Scotty. Besides, it's not just my stuff that's taking up all the space in the spare room.'

He had a point there. This room had also become home to an amazing collection of giant – and I mean giant – papier-mâché puppet heads. Some were girls' heads, some were men. Some had hair, some were bald. Some looked happy. Some looked sad. Some had huge eyes, others were squinting. One even wore a pair of glasses. They'd been made by a chap who, while I was in hospital giving birth to Jordie, had been caught at Bangkok airport with heroin and given twenty-five years in a Bangkok jail. We were all very shocked at the time as none of us had any idea he was into drug-smuggling.

It transpired that this bloke had accumulated some massive debts so his wife, with whom I was friends at the time, was forced to sell their house. She knew about our enormous garage that you couldn't drive a car into and asked if we would do her a big favour and store her husband's puppet heads there because 'he's put so much work and love into making them and he loves them so much and he'll be so happy to see them again when he gets out.' I didn't like to say, 'But that will be in twenty-five years; people's interests do change.' We agreed to take the heads but by this time the garage/big cupboard/shed was full and thus they were stored in the spare room. Eventually, the wife moved on with her life and divorced her husband while he was still in jail. However, John and I continued to dutifully store those heads.

One night when we were at our children's primary school concert, I looked across the foyer and saw him –

the owner of the puppet heads. He wandered over and said, 'Hi Scotty, hi John.'

'Hi, how are you?' I replied, not knowing what else to say. Well, I knew what I *wanted* to say but I figured blurting out something like, 'My godfather, what the hell are you doing here? Why aren't you still in jail in Bangkok?' would have been somewhat tactless and insensitive. It turned out he'd got a king's pardon and was released early. Not that he told us this; I found out later. We continued to make small talk and he explained that he was a friend of one of the mums at the school. At no point did he come even close to asking, 'Hey, you don't happen to know what became of my giant papier-mâché puppet heads do you?' In fact, I got the distinct impression that he probably hadn't given those heads a single moment's thought in a very long time.

'Oh well, at least now we can get rid of those puppet heads, John.'

'Not yet, Scotty. I'm saving them for next year's Fringe Festival parade.'

I was defeated. For now.

CHAPTER 10

Big Gig leads to big fear leads to big change leads to big top leads to ... whatever it was, it was big

t had to happen – being hippie types who enjoyed a bit of social experimentation, John and I were destined to give the old role-reversal a go at some point in our relationship. John would stay at home and look after the house and kids while I would earn the money. What could be more straightforward than that? Almost anything, as it turned out.

At approximately 8.45 pm one Tuesday I found myself pacing the gloomy, hospital-like corridor of the ABC television studios in Elsternwick. Numerous other comics were engaged in the same ritual, walking up and down, up and down, up and down, all the while incessantly muttering to themselves like demented folk in the lock-up ward of an insane asylum. I spotted comedian Rachel Berger coming out of the ladies' toilet. She was wearing her trademark gold shimmery retro top, big bauble earrings, tight black pants and a pair of '50s-style high-heeled shoes. Our eyeballs locked; they were wide-eyed and unblinking. Rachel then uttered a phrase that emblazoned itself forever upon my brain: 'Scotty, you can smell the stink of fear in the toilets.'

I nodded in acknowledgement and we both about-faced and continued pacing. The 'stink of fear' had absolutely nothing to do with one's bowel and everything to do with the fact that each one of us in that corridor was about to walk into a television studio and perform live to air a routine we had never previously tried in public. And there was always the possibility that it would indeed stink. I caught Rachel's eye again. I said something like, 'It feels like we're Christians waiting to be thrown to the lions, don't you reckon?'

'Scotty, I'm Jewish,' Rachel said, and kept walking.

I had just become a regular cast member on a show called *The Big Gig* which, in the late '80s and early '90s, was broadcast from the ABC studios every Tuesday at 9.30 pm. By the time I joined the show during its second series, it had already proved a huge success, making folk like Jean Kittson, Wendy Harmer and the Doug Anthony All Stars household names. The performers were required to write their own material each week. I came to the show with pretty much nothing in my kitbag except the stink of fear and a vague idea that I'd essentially 'borrowed' from elsewhere. It was a sketch I used to watch on TV when I was a kid, where Australian comedian Dawn Lake would talk to a chap in drag over a fence. It was the only idea I had, and that's why I love Jean Kittson because she agreed to write and perform the 'women over the fence' sketch with me. It was like having the head prefect of an exclusive girls' school, who had perfect hair and teeth, choose the scholarship girl from a poor family, who wore a hand-me-down uniform and stockings darned with wool, to accompany her in the stretch limo to the school social.

That first week I appeared on *The Big Gig*, our 'women over the fence' went well so the director asked us to do another the following week. What? Was he crazy? Was he for real? Another one? Come off it. How was I meant to think up another idea? I simply didn't have one. Hell, so this is what it meant to actually work as a comedian? Jesus, what a shocking, slap-in-the-face wake-up call this was.

The next Monday morning, I arrived at the ABC fully expecting to take fear and self-doubt to new and unexplored depths – and I didn't disappoint myself. Jean felt much the same. We had to admit our second 'women over the fence' script wasn't up to scratch.

We opened the heavy, soundproof door and stepped into the dark, cavernous world of studio 32 for a camera rehearsal. Here we would rehearse our sketch but purely for the benefit of the camera crew. They would use this time to work out their angles and shots. 'It's purely for the cameramen. It's purely for the cameramen. It's purely for the cameramen.' This mantra was going through my head as Jean and I took up our positions on either side of the makeshift corrugated fence.

'It's purely for the cameramen,' Jean whispered to me as those four minutes of camera rehearsal stretched into an eternity of overwhelming silence.

'I know, Jean,' I whispered back, 'it's purely for the cameramen.'

But if that were the case, how come when the Doug Anthony All Stars rocked up for their rehearsal (all pelvic-thrusting, testosterone-driven, irreverent characters that they were) they had those very same cameramen laughing until they couldn't speak, laughing until they wheezed and had tears streaming down their faces? And then there was Ted, the director. Jean had warned me that he rarely laughed during rehearsals. But give him the Doug Anthonys – and I saw it with my own eyes – he grinned and then, oh my God, could it be? Ted was laughing. Audibly laughing! Oh horrid, depressing day. Oh, unfunny ladies.

My only consolation was that Jean was famous from *The Big Gig*; everyone acknowledged that she was a brilliant comedian. As long as I stuck with her, hung onto her coat-tails like grim death, it couldn't be that bad, surely. Oh yes, it could! Oh God, this was suicidal stuff.

Why did I ever think a story about a sausage sizzle would be funny? Sausage sizzles are not funny. Sausage sizzles are not hip. Sausage sizzles aren't sexy. Sausage sizzles are boring. But sausage sizzle was all I'd been able to come up with. The primary school had held one the week before. But as great writers have often been heard to say, 'Just because it happened doesn't make it interesting.' But it was too late for such realisations, we had our four minutes scheduled and the following night we would walk out to face the lions and be eaten alive.

Tuesday evening Jean and I paced that corridor, the stink of fear wafting and weaving and curling and seeping into every pore, every crack, every part of my being. I muttered my lines: 'I've always enjoyed having a nibble on an exotic sausage; I'll even accommodate a bratwurst at a stretch. Hell, give me any sausage and I'll give it a go …' Oh, Jesus Christ.

At 9.30 pm Jean and I were standing by in our costumes. Mine was a pink floral flannelette nightie with a bri-nylon dressing gown; Jean's was an old windcheater and trackie daks. We shook hands. We reassured one another, 'Look, it's only four minutes of our entire lives … we all fail sometimes. It's taking the risk that's important. Yes, we may well die out there tonight but tomorrow we'll resurrect ourselves.' Who were we kidding? We both looked ill. Quite ill.

The countdown to showtime began. The audience was yelling in unison, 'TEN, NINE, EIGHT …' Oh

God, the show had started. Brilliant, confident, razor-sharp Wendy Harmer delivered her opening monologue. She kicked goal after comedy goal. The audience roared their approval. Flacco then had the audience in hysterics with some surreal piece of comedy genius. The crowd adored him and whooped and hollered; he could do no wrong. Then it was our turn. Jean and I stepped up to the fence in silence. The studio audience was watching some pre-taped footage on a large monitor. The first assistant director held his finger in the air. The moment that finger came down our shame would start. I watched that finger, wishing/hoping/praying for an earthquake that would prevent its dropping. But alas, it dropped, and Jean and I started the sausage-sizzle routine.

But hark! What was that I could hear? Laughter! Big, fat, gorgeous laughter. It seemed sausages were amusing after all. The laughter grew. This was ridiculous. It was insane. It was shocking. Jean and I looked at each other and were quite literally so astounded by the sound of laughter that we lost it. We laughed too. We couldn't stop, which is fun when you're having a catch-up with a girlfriend at a bar or a coffee-shop, but we were on live television. With every ounce of discipline I could muster, I willed myself not to laugh. I pictured my dad in his coffin the night of the viewing. But to no avail. Jean and I were gone. Our four-minute nightmare extended into eight minutes of Jean and I trying to pull ourselves together, regain our composure and get through the script. The harder we tried to stop laughing, the more we laughed, and the more we laughed, the more the audience laughed. And it was funny. It was more than funny. It was liberating. It was a triumph ...

... for a minute. But then there was the next week's show to think about, and once more I resumed worrying and wondering how I was going to be able to do it.

It was during this rollercoaster, stink of fear, uncertain, *Big Gig* period that John and I agreed that he would stay home and look after the house and kids while I would go to work and earn the money. The first problem with this arrangement was that I didn't actually 'go out' to work very often. Most of the time I was at home trying to write in the non-Zen, still-full-of-other-people's-crap spare room. House-husband John saw this situation as a good opportunity to do something he hadn't had the time to do while he was at work, namely go to the gym. 'Won't be long, Scotty. I'll just do a few laps, a quick workout, and I won't have a spa today, promise.'

Then there was the unexpected complication that saw me downright refusing to relinquish my matriarchal crown. Who would've thought I'd hang on to it with all the tenacity of a highly agitated pit bull terrier? I'd always firmly believed that I couldn't wait for the day when I was no longer responsible for all the domestic duties; and yet, come the day ...

'I'm going shopping, Scotty, any requests?'

'Don't worry, John; I'll do the shopping tomorrow.'

'Why? I'll take the kids with me and we'll get it done today.'

'I'd rather do it tomorrow.'

'That's stupid. You've got to work. Why don't I just do it today?'

'Because I want to do it.'

'Why?'

'It relaxes me, and to be honest, I don't like the fruit you buy.'

'What's wrong with the fruit I buy?'

'Those apples you bought yesterday were bruised.'

'Only a couple of them; anyway, they tasted good.'

'I thought they were disgusting.'

'Alright then. At least let me get some food for tonight's dinner. You do like the food I cook, don't you?

'Yeah, I guess so but …'

'What?'

'Does it always have to be such an event? Last night that Moroccan feast …'

'Didn't you like it?'

'It was great, but John, the kids need to eat before midnight.'

Then there was the way John hung out the clothes.

'Are you saying that I don't peg the clothes on the line the same way as you and therefore I should change my method?'

'No, John, I'm not saying that at all. It's the way you do it, with all that pomp and circumstance, the way you parade through the house huffing and puffing and drawing attention to yourself: "Oh, look at me, I'm carrying another basket of washing to the line. Aren't I amazing?" Can't you just do it quietly like I do?'

'But Scotty, I am not you. I do things differently.'

'Well, how about showing some respect for the fact that I've been hanging out the clothes for the last five years and asking me for advice on the best way to do it?'

Then there was the tug-of-war as to who would pay the bills.

'I'll fix them up, Scotty.'

'No, I'll do it.'

'Why?'

'Because John, I know you'll be late.'

'No, Scotty, it's because I know you want control.'

On the other hand, John was thrilled to finally have the time to join the kindergarten committee. He was the only man. He loved it, and no wonder. How many people can say they've regularly come home from kinder committee meetings after midnight, reeking of alcohol and marijuana? And the fundraiser we had that year: a huge dinner-dance for which John booked the hall, organised the band, set up a crèche at the kinder for the night, and cooked Indian curry and rice for 250 people.

But what excited John most about being a house-husband was that he finally fulfilled a long-held dream and started his own children's community circus. It was called the Little Big Tops and Bonnie and Jordie were the first to join. They had no choice, such was the fate of children sprung from the loins of a circus-lovin' dad whose idea of a top day out was marching in a street parade wearing a full-body lycra snakeskin leotard and bashing a soup ladle against a colander that was strapped upside down on his head.

Thus, by the age of five Bonnie could lie on her stomach and bend her legs backwards over her body until her little bare feet came to rest on top of her head; and Jordie, who was seven, could confidently ride a unicycle while playing a small guitar. (Jordie has since claimed that his years in the circus have really come in handy as an adult. Apparently the when-I-was-a-kid-I-was-in-my-dad's-circus line is a great ice-breaker when chatting up the ladies.)

Almost immediately, the Little Big Tops took on a life of its own. Portable trapeze rigs had to be built, tightrope equipment and crash-mats purchased, specialty trainers employed, and a parents' committee formed to help run the enterprise. There were hat-making working bees, costume-making working bees, stilt-making working bees, stilt-pants-making working bees, twirling-ribbons-on-sticks-making working bees, and catering working bees to provide food for those participating in working bees. Parents volunteered their time and experience to do rigging, lights, make-up and music. As much as I resented John spending so much time with the circus and so little time with me, I had to acknowledge that it seemed to give parents and kids alike a sense of belonging to a community and I didn't want to miss out. That's why I initially attempted to help John in the training sessions. Until the incident with Brigid.

John was getting the kids to do an exercise he'd learnt from the Nanjing Acrobats of China. In this particular stretch, the kids had to stand with their backs against a wall with their feet a little way forward. They would then slowly slide their backs down the wall until they were in a sitting position. They then had to hold this position for what seemed like a really long time. Actually, it didn't *seem* like a long time, it *was* a long time, an excruciatingly long time. In fact, I'd go so far as to say that having to sit without a chair to hold you up can be one of the slowest sixty seconds of one's life.

I was assisting a tiny six-year-old girl named Brigid. She was gorgeous. She had fair skin with tiny freckles across her little button nose, bright blue eyes and red curly hair. She had slid down the wall and was in the sitting position when she whispered ever so quietly to me, 'It's hurting, Miss.'

'I know it's hurting, but it's meant to. Hang in there; you're doing a great job.'

'But Miss, it's really, really hurting.'

'I know. But if you want to become a good acrobat,' which I'm pretty sure at that particular moment would not have been at the top of Brigid's 'Things I Must Do

Before I Die' list, 'you have to move through the pain barrier. Apparently it's all the go in China.'

By now Brigid's face was contorted in such a way that I suspected she was on the verge of tears. I continued my motivational pep-talk, 'You are being so brave, come on, hold it just a little bit longer.'

Finally, John announced that all the kids could stand up straight. As Brigid stepped away from the wall, that's when I saw it – a nail that had been hammered through from the other side, its pointy bit jutting out just where little Brigid's back had been. That poor little freckle-faced, red-headed kid; she'd just endured her own scaled-down version of a crucifixion. I felt awful, but I felt even worse when I remembered that her father was a federal politician.

The circus began to consume more and more and even more time. There were more and more and even more bookings for festival appearances. I was becoming more and more and even more resentful, but what could I say? Sure, I could have said something along the lines of, 'John, could you please abandon the 150 or so people who now rely on you to give their difficult lives some meaning, hope and joy; not to mention the kids who, until the circus, had struggled to fit in anywhere; not to mention the one severely disabled girl who had shone and dazzled with her special wheelchair routine; not to mention the disabled girl's mother who'd wept with gratitude; not to mention the 'blended' family whose step-kids overcame their resentment of one another while performing a juggling routine together; not to mention the estranged, alcoholic father who'd stopped drinking and re-united with his kids because the circus made use of his welding skills and he simply blossomed; not to mention the thousands of people who'd been moved to tears watching these little kids proudly march down a suburban street on their stilts, joyfully waving to the crowd as they passed. Yes, anyway, John, as I was saying, if you could just abandon all these people and come home and cook dinner because I have to write a four-minute comedy sketch and I've only got a week to do it ...'

I began to view life differently. I would watch a film like *Gandhi* and all I could think was, 'Oh, it's all well and good for Mahatma to head off and save millions of poor and dying Indians but what about his wife?' Whenever I saw a large crowd on the TV cheering and applauding some world leader who'd just made a speech promising not to rest until peace and equality had been achieved, all I could imagine was that male leader's wife in a nearby public toilet weeping with exhaustion.

'I can't stand it, John.'

'What?'

'You're running around the place like some guru.'

'Scotty, I'm not trying to be a guru.'

'But that's how people see you. You're the all-knowing one. "Oh John, where do you want the hemline to be for the kids' pants in the roller-boller routine?"; "Oh John, how many layers of balloons do I need to make juggling balls and how much rice?"; "John, how do you tune a ukulele?" And then there's that mum, Fiona, "Oh John, could you come over here and hold my hand while I have a go at walking on stilts? Oh, thank you so much, John. Do you think you could help me get off the stilts now?" It makes me sick watching you help some hot mother get off her stilts.'

'Well, what was I meant to do?'

'As far as I'm concerned, you should have left her on them for the rest of her life.'

It must be said that stilts, in general, were giving me the shits. As the parent of a child stilt–walker, it was expected that you would discreetly walk beside them in a parade and assist them if they fell. If this unfortunate situation occurred (and it always did) you could simply tell your child to put their hands around your neck and then you'd drag them along behind you until you found a suitable place to try to stand them up again. It was this experience that prompted me to observe that any parent who claimed they enjoyed watching the Moomba Parade had clearly never had to help their own child walk down Swanston Street on a pair of stilts.

Never did that stretch of road seem so endless, so eternal, so like the Nullarbor, stretching on and on and on. Oh, at the start of the parade it was all squeals and laughter and joking as the kids set off with their long, brightly coloured pants and big, tall, funny foam hats; but by Lonsdale Street this merriment was replaced by despair, anxiety and exhaustion.

'Are we there yet? My legs are hurting.'

'Come on, keep going. Only another three kilometres to go.'

At the end of this particular parade, all the kids were lying on the grass outside the Arts Centre. Parents were massaging their children's cramped little legs and providing drinks and snacks. That's when we heard the announcement: 'The winner for Best Community Group in the Moomba Parade is … the Little Big Tops!' This was great news until John explained to us that, as part of the prize, we had to do a lap of honour around the Alexandra Gardens – on stilts.

'You've got be joking. This is insane, completely insane. It's ridiculous. It's cruelty to children, I'm going to kill John when we get home for putting me and my kids through this hell. Another fucking lap? They can't be serious,' I muttered and cursed as I tied Bonnie's stilts back on.

John yelled, 'Okay kids, is everybody ready? Off we go.' Saucepan lids were banged together, creating the primitive, rhythmic, percussive beat that signalled it was time to head 'em up and move 'em out. That's when Bonnie said, 'Mum, I need to go to the toilet.' I looked at her, willing her not to be serious.

'Oh God, can't you hang on?'

'No.' She looked as though she was about to burst into tears which was understandable; it's bad enough to wet your pants in public, but to wet them from a great height ...

'It's alright, Bonn, don't worry,' I said in a clearly tense, what–the–hell–are–we–going–to–do, worried–sick sort of voice.

'Come on, I'll take off your stilts and we'll find a toilet.'

'Mum, there isn't time, it's coming!'

Oh God, oh Jesus Christ, where? Where in God's name is there a toilet in the city? And then I saw it. The Arts Centre spire. 'Come on, Bonnie.'

We took off at great speed. Bonnie was impressive, effortlessly weaving in and out of the crowd on her tall stilts. We hurried into the foyer of the great concert hall where, much to my dismay, there was a sea of white hair and walking frames. A senior citizens' concert was about to start.

'Excuse me, I'm sorry, um excuse me, can we get through?'

A couple of women in their eighties turned around and began to crankily berate me for being rude and pushing in. Their heads slowly looked up until they caught sight of Bonnie's head standing a good metre and a half above them. I explained, 'I'm sorry but my daughter's in a hurry to go to ...'

'Off you go, darling.' And they made room for us to pass. I heard one of them say, 'It must be all the hormones in the chicken ... It's a joke, Beryl. Oh, forget it.'

Bonnie and I arrived at the toilet to find a long queue. All of these elderly women accepted without question that Bonnie needed to go in a desperate hurry and it was they who insisted she move to the head of the line. Knowing from my own mum and her friends just how weak an elderly woman's bladder could be, I appreciated their generosity.

Finally, Bonnie and I were in the cubicle. Now what? Having to lower a child onto a toilet seat when they've got six-foot legs that don't bend isn't easy. Bonnie stood in front of the toilet bowl and I stood facing her. She bent over slightly and put both her hands on my head to balance herself. In this position I managed to get Bonn's pants down. She then bent further forward, wrapped both arms around my neck and slowly slid down until she was seated on the toilet bowl and her stilts were sticking out the bottom of the toilet door. I heard one old lady trip over them and jokingly say, 'Oh well, there goes my hip.'

Eventually, Bonnie and I caught up with the others at the Moomba Parade award ceremony in the gardens. Fiona, the hot stilt-walking mum, came over to me. Hugging me, she said, 'Isn't this great? You must be so proud of that husband of yours.' She looked over at John in his lycra leotard who, at that very moment, performed a spontaneous celebratory cartwheel. 'Isn't he amazing?'

'Yes,' I replied and wanted to vomit.

'Where does he get all his energy from and is he always this happy?' I knew what she really wanted to say was, 'And is he always this happy as opposed to you, you miserable, bitter, resentful bitch.'

I headed off to the nearby public toilets on my own. They were pretty disgusting but they offered privacy and solitude and a place for some peaceful contemplation of life. Once I was locked safely inside the cubicle, I sat down on the cold, grey, metal bowl and would have burst into a rendition of Shannon Noll's version of 'What about me? It isn't fair ...' but that song was still at least fifteen years away from being recorded so I burst into tears instead. (During this period, had I been asked, I would have declared 'spontaneous weeping' a favourite pastime.) I had a quiet word with God, who rarely ever heard from me. But I needed to talk to someone and I couldn't honestly say I'd ever had anything to do with Buddha or Yahweh or Allah so good old Catholic God it was.

'Dear God, how come role-reversal means that I now go out and work to earn the family income and yet it seems I still do the shopping, the cooking, the cleaning, the washing and the organising of the birthday parties and presents? I know, God, I know, I know, I know that it seems like I want to do everything at home and I sort of do but I want help. I need help. I'm so tired, God, but on top of everything else I have to support John's projects; it's the only way I can get to see him and the kids and what really pisses me off is that I have to put up with attractive, young, single − or for that matter attached but desperately unhappy – mothers going on and on about how amazing John is.'

I sat in that stinking toilet waiting, but there was no response. Fair enough. If I was God and had to choose between listening to me crying about some issues with children juggling balls or a mother weeping about her child dying of starvation I wouldn't have chosen me. All I could hear as I continued to sit and weep on that toilet bowl was the carnival music promising a good time for all the family.

'Oh well, Scotty,' (since God was busy elsewhere I was now forced to talk to myself) 'at least you've got a good idea for next week's "women over the fence" sketch.' I wondered if I should change Fiona's name.

CHAPTER 11

A bumpy ride into the eye of a storm

was standing underneath the Hills hoist. It was 5.15 pm. I was wearing my dressing gown over the top of my bra and pants, knee-high stockings and high-heeled black boots. Uncharacteristically, I was wearing make-up, including eye-shadow, eyeliner and a vivid red lipstick, which I bought because it was called 'rich and famous'. Could the mere name of a lipstick influence your future? One could only hope. I was managing to suck on a Benson and Hedges 16 mg cigarette without the use of my arms or hands. They were busy removing clothes from the line. I stumbled back across our yard, ducking to avoid a cricket ball that had been hit by Jordie, bowled by his friend Josh.

'Can we go back on the clothesline now, Mum?'

'Yes, okay.'

They walked back towards the clothesline where they resumed swinging from bike tubes that John had ingeniously tied onto the steel arms of the hoist, so that they resembled large elastic bands.

'Can you give us a spin, Mum?'

I put down the clothes basket, went back to the line, grabbed the broom handle which was purposely placed nearby, and positioned it in such a way that when I ran around the base of the Hills hoist it helped spin the clothesline so the kids, dangling upside down from their tubes, went flying out to the side.

I then picked up the clothes basket again, headed towards the back door, butted out my cigarette, came into the kitchen, threw the basket onto the floor, and walked past Bonnie, who was busy at her workstation. That kid was addicted to her cutting and pasting sessions. I went into my bedroom and had a couple of squirts of Ventolin. I preferred to do this procedure in private as I didn't want the children to know that my wheezing was bad because they might associate the problem with my smoking, and then they might give me looks of disdain, which might then force me to give up cigarettes, which at that point in my life would've most certainly killed me.

So, having had my secret squirt of Ventolin, I was now back in the kitchen. I looked at our old Roman numeral clock that we bought for $3 at the local auction rooms. It would've been a great buy except we dropped it and broke the glass face the same day we bought it. It was 5.20 pm. I headed towards the bench, sighing deeply. Bonnie looked up, her little face alarmed, for she knew that this particular tight, sucking sort of sighing was different from the normal, everyday sigh and was, in fact, a method I used to warn the family that all was not well.

I started chopping vegetables with our old meat-cleaver, which had a huge split in the wooden handle, which John had fixed in the same way he fixed everything – with gaffer tape. Every time I used it, I heard my mother's words: 'When I was doing my nurses' aide training, we once got to look at a cracked cup under a microscope and the number of germs teeming with life in that crack ... I've never used anything with a crack or a chip in it since.' In contrast to my mum, I liked to believe that a germ-filled house would build up the kids' immune system. I looked at the clock again: 5.25 pm. John should be home any minute. His days as a house-husband were in the past and he now had paid work as an event organiser of local festivals. I was back doing freelance stand-up comedy gigs. 5.26. Oh, come on, John. I started chopping the carrots with more frenzy than was necessary. What if John's late? Was I crazy? What *if* John's late? Of course he was going to be late. He was always late. Now I was worried sick. I asked myself the big question: Why? Why had I ever accepted a gig doing stand-up comedy for the men who make briquettes? Then I remembered. Of course, it was for the money. But why on earth would they ever have chosen a female comedian to entertain the men who make briquettes? Then I remembered. It was because the previous year they had a male comic who swore big time and the briquette boss's wife was so offended she got up and walked out. I started to run through my routine, muttering quietly to myself: 'I remember when I was a kid the briquette man always came on a Tuesday, wearing his little shorts, his big muscular arms holding the bag of briquettes on his broad, strong, sweaty shoulders. I know it was a Tuesday because that was the day my mother would wear a mini-skirt and lipstick.' I told myself that, okay, it mightn't be funny but at least I wasn't using the word 'cunt'.

5.48 pm. Where the hell was John? He had to be home in twelve minutes, at which point I would then call a cab, which, fingers crossed, wouldn't take any longer than ten minutes to arrive, which meant that I could be in Ripponlea by approximately 6.50 pm in time to collect myself and be on stage at 7.15 pm. But what if there were hassles with traffic? What if there were delays on Punt Road? Maybe the back way via Kew was better. But what if the taxi-driver didn't know the way? What if he got lost? 5.51 pm. My stomach was now in a giant knot. I threw the vegetables into a casserole pot, I threw a chook on top and then I threw the whole catastrophe into the oven. I raced back down the hall and into the bedroom, threw off my dressing gown and threw on my suit.

5.58 pm. The phone rang. It couldn't be John ringing to say he was running late, could it? Surely he wasn't that predictable?

'Sorry Scotty ...'

'John, where are you?'

'In Preston.'

'In the car?'

'No, I'm at Nick's.'

'Who's Nick?

'He runs a small grocers' shop.'

'But you're meant to be home. I've got this corporate gig.'

'I know, I know. I'll be there soon.'

'When?'

'Five minutes.'

'John, you can't make it from Preston in five minutes ...'

'I can, but alright, make it seven minutes. No seriously, I reckon I can be there in six and a half.'

'But John, I have to leave now ...'

'Okay, call the cab and by the time it gets there I'll be home.'

'But what if you're not?'

'Well, you can head off. The kids will be fine on their own for a few minutes.'

'John, I'm not leaving the kids on their own and why the hell are you at a grocers'?'

'Well, see, Nick's part of the Macedonian community and there's been a drama with the street parade this

Saturday because I organised for the Macedonians to gather in the same marshalling area as the Greeks and now the Macedonians are saying they may have to withdraw, so I'm just trying to sort something out ...'

'Are you trying to tell me that you're attempting to solve the Greek–Macedonian conflict?'

'Well, sort of ...'

'Fuck the Greek–Macedonian conflict, John, what about me? It's six o'clock. What am I going to do? My material about men who sell briquettes is shit; I'm going to be late. It's too hard ... I can't do this anymore, John.'

'You'll be great, Scotty.'

'How will I be great, John? At this rate I probably won't even get there. What am I going to do?'

'Scotty, I'm going to get in the car now. I'll be out the front in a few minutes. I'll toot the horn. We'll put the kids in the car and I'll drive you to Ripponlea.'

I turned down the casserole and yelled at the kids: 'Kids, come on. Dad's picking us up and we're all going in the car.'

'Where?'

'Your father's taking me to my gig.'

'Do we have to come?'

'Yes, you do.'

'Why?'

I heard the car horn tooting out the front.

'Just get in the car.'

'But Mum, Josh is still here. Can we drop Josh off at his place?'

'No, there isn't time. Josh, you get in the car too. You'll have to come with us.'

We all climbed in the car. John had left the engine running but had got out of the car and raced inside the house. I wound down the window.

'John, what in God's name are you doing now?'

'I've just got to get something ...'

'John, please do not do this. I'm going to be late.'

But John had disappeared into the house. A couple of minutes passed. I got out of the car and headed back inside. I stood in the hallway and screamed: 'JOHN!'

He came flying out of the spare room with a big sack over his shoulder. We both ran back to the car. John threw the sack into the boot. We jumped into the car and off we screeched. In the best possible circumstances, I would now arrive at the gig just one minute before I was due on stage.

We were almost at Kew Junction before I unclenched my gritted teeth and asked, 'So what's in the sack, John?'

'Just some old saucepans and drums.'

'And you needed to put them in the boot now?'

'Well, yeah. I thought that seeing as I'm heading over towards St Kilda, I may as well drop the saucepan lids into Tom's.'

'Why?'

'Because he's running a percussion workshop with a

group of disabled kids this weekend. Do you have a problem with that, Scotty?'

'Oh, goodness me, no. No problem at all, John, no problem at all.'

John and I may as well have scripted that argument; we seemed to repeat it on a daily basis. But we were on the cusp of change at number 26. We were about to sail into calmer waters where both John and I would have regular jobs, the house would be clean, the kids would be calm and there would be a homemade meal on the table every night at 6.30 pm. Now this may imply that at some point John and I had had a moment of Oprah Winfrey realisation where, with tears welling in our eyes and our voices quavering with emotion, we had looked at each other and said, 'We can't go on living like this. It's tearing our family apart. We have to do something and if that means we have to change, then by golly we will do it, we'll change our lives, no matter how hard it is.' And the worldwide audience of millions would've applauded our courage and Oprah would've wiped tears from her eyes and said something like, 'Wow!' And John and I would've sobbed and hugged each other.

But none of this happened. In the dullness that is reality, John and I had simply continued to roll along and it just turned out that life took us to a relatively tranquil place; but getting there was by no means a straightforward process.

Around this time I got a gig on *Tonight Live*. It was a live variety show hosted by Steve Vizard that screened five nights a week on Channel Seven. I appeared in a weekly segment called 'Clean Up Your Act'. It was a *Beauty and the Beast*–style panel featuring four female panellists from varying backgrounds. Originally there had been another female comic in the line-up but she had decided that it wasn't her thing so at the last minute they'd rung me to replace her.

'Okay, now Denise, you will be on tomorrow night's show which, for various reasons, has to be pre-recorded at 4 pm tomorrow. This means you will have to be at the studio for make-up and camera rehearsal at 1 pm. Can you make that?'

'Sure, I can.'

'Great, Denise. Thanks so much for helping us out.'

'Not a problem.' (Helping them out! Didn't they know I had no other paid income to speak of?)

But there *was* a problem. A big problem. When I got that phone call I wasn't in Melbourne. I was in Mallacoota, which is a long, long, long way from Melbourne. I was there to perform my one-woman show in the Mallacoota Mudbrick Arts Pavilion that evening. And hey, I don't normally brag, but let's just say in a swaggering kind of way that I had sold out. Yes, indeedy! This was a welcome change as I had just done a two-week season in Sydney at the Belvoir Street Theatre where, on the nights when it wasn't cancelled, I was performing to approximately four people.

John and the kids were in Mallacoota with me and we

were staying at a friend's house. This was tricky. Somehow I had to get back to Melbourne by 1 pm the following day. What to do? What to do?

I did the one thing that is only possible in a small country town — I put the word out. Any sign of strife in the Australian bush and people come running; Mallacoota was no exception. Within an hour of the news of my plight spreading through the town, a middle-aged fisherman with salt-encrusted, dull blond hair and a leathery-brown suntan turned up on our doorstep offering salvation. He was flying his plane to Melbourne the following morning and could deliver me by midday to Moorabbin airport. Was I in the middle of a fairytale? He seemed pretty excited too, very excited, extremely excited ... if you get my drift. I hadn't picked up on his excitement until I witnessed his devastating disappointment when I told him that John and the kids could now fly with us as a friend had offered to drive our car back to Melbourne.

Early the next morning John, Jordie, Bonnie and I stood near the runway at the Mallacoota airstrip. We were beside ourselves with anticipation. Pretty soon I heard a pathetic kind of chug-chugging sound in the distance and looked up into the expansive blue sky. That's when I realised I'd never really seen a light plane before. As that tiny speck headed in to land on the runway, the thing that surprised me most was that it never got much bigger. My godfather, you've got to be joking. How could you fly in anything that small?

Now, there are times in your life when, out of the blue, you learn something about yourself that you never knew before. This was one of them. I learnt that I had an overwhelming, sickening, deep-seated fear of small planes. This phobia had obviously been lying dormant deep within my psyche, just waiting for the day when, for the first time in my life, I was about to board such an aircraft.

The fisherman loaded us in. Bonnie (who was seven at the time) and I (who was about thirty-eight at the beginning of the flight and about one hundred by the end) were sent to the back of the plane, which was only about half a metre from the front. Jordie (who was nine) sat in front of Bonnie and me, next to a young Mallacoota girl who'd heard about the plane offer and had jumped on board as she needed to get back to Melbourne University. John enthusiastically sat up front like a ridiculously happy boy scout, next to the fisherman/pilot. It was at this point that the fisherman looked more disappointed than ever. I guess he was still getting over the fact that his sky-high sexual fantasy of the two of us having a Lauren Bacall–Humphrey Bogart, *Casablanca*-style love tryst over a joystick 18,000 feet up in the air wasn't going to happen. The crestfallen pilot then informed us that he was going to have to drop off mail at various properties on the way. 'Is that a problem for anyone?'

'No,' I managed to murmur from my catatonic state of utter dread.

And so we took off. We swooped and rose and dropped and swooped and bumped up and bumped down and swooped some more and suddenly dropped a bit and then rose up again and continued to rise and whoopsa- daisy, another big bump and oh, fuck me dead, why in God's name did I drink a bottle of red wine last night and then oh, sweet Jesus, hold on to your hats and mittens, kids, because no sooner were we up a long, long way in the air than holy Hannah we were hurtling towards our first paddock to drop off a package and that's when I did my first vomit and that's when I think the last vestige of our trusted pilot's sexual feelings for me disappeared forever. Oh, how many times we ascended ... only to descend again. The flight, which was meant to take about an hour and a half, took four.

It was about an hour into the trip that Bonnie started to vomit. Jordie kicked in at about the two-hour mark. At one point all three of us were vomiting into the one remaining airsick bag at the same time. The poor young uni student had then started doing some sympathetic vomiting. Meanwhile, up in the cockpit, John was having the time of his life. He and the fisherman were getting along like a house on fire and at this point John had actually taken over the controls. 'Have a look at me, Scotty, I'm flying a plane!' In my weakened state I was still able to muster the sarcasm required to drip from the words, 'Gee John, that's fantastic,' before returning my head to the sickbag where I hurled for the eighty-fifth time.

Finally, after what seemed like a year of hell, we landed at Moorabbin airport. I left the fisherman and John to their enthusiastic embracing.

'See ya, Johnny.'

'Yeah, see ya. And hey, thanks a million for the flying lessons.'

'No probs, mate. You were a bloody natural. Brilliant. Can't believe you've never done it before. We'll have to do it again sometime.'

As for me, I had staggered across the tarmac and found a small piece of dusty earth. Planes were landing nearby. I didn't care. I vomited once more and then lay down. I wanted to feel that piece of solid ground beneath me. I was shaking and moaning audibly in that I'm-too-sick-to-care-if-people-hear-me sort of way. John rang a cab to take me to the studio. I arrived looking ... well, looking like someone who shouldn't be appearing on national television. But if there's anyone on this earth who can get you through an emergency, it's the girls from the TV make-up room. I don't know what drugs they gave me but they were brilliant. And they covered my pale, washed-out face with a thick layer of life-giving foundation, did my hair, and on to the studio floor they pushed me.

But sometimes make-up girls can't save the day, and in fact sometimes they can come perilously close to ruining your life, especially if you are about to host a national television show for the first time.

Steve Vizard had gone on holidays for two weeks and I got a call asking if I'd be a fill-in host. Hosting a tonight show! Me! Oh, wow! This was just sensationally unbelievable. I rang my mother: 'Mum, guess what? I'm going to be hosting *Tonight Live* for two weeks!'

After a pause, my mum said, 'Good God, Denise, do you really think you're ready for that?'

It's necessary to clarify that I wasn't going to be hosting on my own. I was to co-host with another 'Clean Up Your Act' panellist, the young and beautiful Sofie Formica. Barb, one of the make-up and hair people from Channel Seven, had offered to perm my hair in her salon on Toorak Road. It has to be understood and accepted (although it may be difficult) that big curly perms were considered attractive then, and in fact Barb did a great job. I loved it. My hair was dyed a gorgeous deep red and I had shoulder-length loose curls. I was happy.

On that first night of hosting I rocked up to the Channel Seven make-up room a bundle of sickening nerves. Barb wasn't working. Another make-up artist, let's just call her Dippy, applied my make-up and all was fine with the world. I was about to vacate the chair to concentrate on the task ahead of me when Dippy said, 'And what will we do with your hair, Denise? It's so curly. Would you like me to straighten it?'

I explained that I'd just spent a great deal of money and time having it curled so, 'No, I don't want it straightened, thanks.'

'Okay,' she responded in her clipped, nasal, everything's-under-control voice. 'Let's see ...' She stepped back and studied me from all angles with an intensity that was truly worrying. 'I know exactly what we need to do,' she announced, and away Dippy went: brushing, pulling, straightening, teasing, spraying until finally she stood back and asked with amazing confidence, 'So, what do you think, Denise?'

Surely my mortified face would've said it all, for Dippy had managed to transform my fabulous loose curl into a hideous, stiff, Princess Margaret bouffant, beehive bun that made me look sixty-five years of age. I said nothing; my grief and devastation were too profound. Besides, I had other things on my mind, such as hosting a live tonight show. That's when Barb, my original hairdresser, arrived in the make-up room to wish me luck.

'God, Denise, your hair! What's happened?' She turned to Dippy, 'What the hell have you done?' Dippy's bottom lip began to quiver. Barb furiously started pulling out all the hairpins. Dippy began to whimper her apologies and tried to help Barb remove the pins. It was now close to quarter-past ten. Fifteen minutes till we were on air. The first assistant director had come to take me to the studio. Barb and Dippy were by now in a frenzy of pulling and yanking and at this point my hair was a kind of big, crazy, teased mess that would have been perfect had I been about to play a woman addicted to speedy diet pills but hey, unfortunately I was about to host a live tonight show.

Twenty-five minutes past nine and the show's executive producer had arrived in the make-up room, yelling, 'What the fuck is going on with Denise's hair?' Talk about calming. By this stage every make-up artist in the building was gathered around me, all grabbing and pulling, while Barb had swung into emergency services mode, yelling instructions. With one minute till we were on air, I ran down the stairs and into the studio and onto the set where I collapsed on the couch. I gazed at my co-host sitting calmly beside me, dressed smartly in her sexy tailored pants and jacket, her straight brown shoulder-length hair shining and her smile radiant. I looked down at my bright-pink retro pants-suit and recalled my weird, ridiculous, tortured-looking bun, and as the ten-second countdown to showtime began, I thought that just maybe my mother was right.

I was then offered a full-time job in the *Tonight Live* writers' room. I searched and searched to find a Buddhist-style quote along the lines of *To go from hosting a live tonight show to the backwaters of its writers' room is not taking a step backwards in one's career; it's merely taking a step in a different direction.* But I've never been able to find it. I did, however, come across this little gem: *If you host a tonight show and it appears that you failed, do not blame yourself, blame your hairdo.*

Being in the writers' room at *Tonight Live* headquarters was the first regular job I'd had since my one and a half years' teaching when I was twenty-two. I knew what time I started. I knew what time I finished. This in turn meant I knew what time I went to bed. I knew what time I got up. It was five days a week. The pay was good and John and I got some help. Steph and Caitlin, both uni students, job-shared picking up Jordie and Bonnie from school and hanging out with them until I got home. This was the beginning, middle and end of their job description but they would also clean up the house, fold the washing, do the dishes and sweep the floor. Their activities with the kids included making homemade pumpkin gnocchi, which would then be left in the fridge along with the homemade napolitana sauce for our dinner. What bliss. What joy. What an unusual sense of everything being right with the world.

Artistically speaking, things couldn't have been less inspiring. I was the only female in the writers' room among seven blokes and I mean *blokes*; at least, the majority of them were blokes. Being in that room was like being on a neverending footy trip. Lunchtime activities included watching full-on porn movies, perving on female guests and making disgusting, sexist comments, which seemed to come to these guys as regularly and easily as breathing. What surprised me was how much I liked them. They were big-hearted and, more importantly, they covered for me and enabled me to keep my job because in the entire year I 'worked' in that room not one thing I wrote ever went to air. Not a syllable. But no one dobbed me in.

On one memorable occasion it was my turn to sit in the studio and watch the rehearsal for that evening's show.

I dreaded this job because you had to sit in the dark in the audience bleachers, and as Steve ran through the show he would suddenly call out, 'Joke, I need a joke here.' And it was your job to provide one on the spot. That particular night I prayed Steve would not make the call but he did. 'Joke, I need a joke.' I froze. My mind was blank. I heard some shuffling in the seats near me. The head writer emerged from the shadows and leant down to whisper a joke in my ear. I yelled the joke to Steve. 'Good work, Denise, thank you,' he said.

John and I managed to save some serious money that year so we decided it was time to renovate number 26. What we didn't know then was that, while it appeared we were existing in a state of relative calm, we were in fact sitting in the eye of a storm.

CHAPTER 12
Pigs might fly

ony Delroy is a late-night broadcaster on ABC radio. At midnight he hosts 'Tony's Quiz', a twenty-five question general knowledge situation where callers ring in and answer the questions, with the winner receiving a gardening magazine in an ABC calico bag. In the mid-'90s John and I became hooked. Every night, without fail, we'd get into bed, turn off the bedside lights, turn on the radio, snuggle under the doona, and between us try to answer Tony's questions. Sometimes we would have been in the kitchen having a screaming argument about issues such as betrayal, deception and infidelity when suddenly one of us would look at the clock and say, 'It's nearly twelve o'clock.' With all the panic of Cinderella at the ball, we would immediately forget our fight and race around, cleaning our teeth, getting

undressed and jumping into bed where Tony's reassuring voice would immediately calm us.

Years later I was doing a fill-in shift on the evening program at the ABC, and as part of the show I would talk to Tony Delroy. One evening while we were chatting on air, I told him that his quiz had helped John and my relationship. He wasn't that surprised. In fact, he went on to tell me that he'd once met a woman who confessed that she and her husband used to make love while listening to his quiz. What a revelation. The thought of Tony's dulcet voice asking what is the capital of Zambia while a sweaty couple at home approaches orgasm, screaming, 'Yes! Yes! Yes, it's Lusaka!' has meant that I've never been able to listen to Tony's quiz in quite the same way since.

John had only recently moved back into number 26; for two months he'd been living at his brother's place. He'd moved out the day after I threw a large piece of marinated pork at his head. As the marinade dripped down his stunned face, bits of parsley and rosemary remaining stuck in his hair, we stood looking at each other, knowing that this was it — we'd hit rock-bottom and something or someone had to give.

Trouble had been brewing and gathering intensity for some time. John's work schedule had become crazier and more stressful than ever. He was directing large festivals as well as continuing to run the Little Big Tops. At one stage he drove under a low bridge in South Melbourne in a high truck he'd hired to transport some festival equipment. The roof peeled off the top of that truck as easily and smoothly as the opening of a sardine tin. John, being in a hurry to get to the festival, simply left the roof by the roadside and continued on his way. It wasn't until the following day that John learnt the hire company's insurance policy didn't cover people driving a truck that is clearly too tall under a bridge that is clearly too low, and we were informed we'd have to pay for a new roof on the truck. Somehow we got out of this debacle but it was a tense couple of weeks.

Meanwhile, I'd been working as a full-time cast member on a comedy show called *Full Frontal*. One Friday afternoon while we were having a few weeks' break from filming before shooting the next series, a courier delivered a letter from the *Full Frontal* production team. (This was not unusual as it was in the days before email.) The letter contained the usual information, including all the starting times and location details for the following Monday. It was the last sentence that was a little out of the norm: 'Unfortunately, Denise Scott has decided to pursue other interests and will not be joining us for the next series.' I read it out to John. 'What do you think that means, John?'

'I think it means you've been sacked, Scotty.'

These were not the best of times.

If further proof were needed that things were a little unhinged at number 26, I provided it by choosing to wear a bare-midriff outfit to my fortieth birthday party, which was held at home. That's right, a bare midriff, beautifully highlighting my white stomach which was covered in moles. When one guest arrived, she poked her finger right into my flesh and said, 'I just had to do that. It's just like mine, all soft and pudgy. I've been going to the gym for years but at our age nothing helps, does it?'

Before the birthday cake was cut, John made a speech that ended with the words, 'Life is a struggle and life with Scotty is a ... magnificent struggle.' The giant mud-cake was topped with cream and strawberries. The candles were lit, happy birthday was sung, it was time to cut the cake. I had the knife poised when my brother-in-law yelled, 'Use the chainsaw!' He'd borrowed it some weeks earlier and had returned it to us that evening, which was why it was sitting in the corner of the living area. I heard my mother's voice in my head: 'All the time and all the effort that's gone into making that cake, not to mention the fortune you paid for it. It would be such a waste.'

I kickstarted the chainsaw. Cake sprayed everywhere. Chocolate and cream splattered the guests, who were screaming and trying to run, but there was nowhere to run to. I felt like Jack Nicholson in *The Shining*, grinning my head off with evil intent as I kept attacking that cake. Okay, some of the guests' outfits were ruined and yes, I'll admit that the bits of cake that were salvaged didn't taste great with all the petrol that had seeped into it; and yes, it was very hard, in fact impossible, to get the cake off the ceiling; and yes, it was a waste. But it was a MAGNIFICENT waste.

A few months later, John held his fortieth birthday party in our backyard. It featured a huge bonfire and guests were asked to bring something to burn as a symbolic gesture of letting go of the old and bringing in the new. John chose to burn his full-length caftan, and as it disappeared in the flames John let out a raw, guttural cry and took a spontaneous leap over the hot coals, strongly indicating that some form of release from the past was taking place.

John then got a job working on a major festival in country Victoria. He was frequently away, and one morning he flew back to Melbourne on a regional flight and called in to see us at home before heading off to his city office. We were all sitting on the bed together when I innocently asked John about the farming family he was supposed to have stayed with the night before. 'Well, actually, Scotty …' It was the word 'actually' that did it. I knew right there and then that John was having an affair. It was that night I threw the pig and the next day John moved out.

It seemed incomprehensible that life had come to this. Jordie and Bonnie were dazed and confused: what had become of their happy, loving, devoted family, where Mum worked in comedy and Dad was a clown?

A few weeks later, a note came home from the school about Bonnie. There was a concern that she appeared to have forgotten how to read or spell. She had to have a series of tests done on her eyes and ears, and for things like dyslexia. They all came back clear. When we told her the news her large eyes welled up with tears. She whispered, 'Then that means I must just be stupid.' I recalled the pork incident and knew without a doubt who the stupid ones were in this scenario.

After John moved out, I did things I'd never done before, such as drink vodka straight from the bottle while lying under the Hills hoist in the foetal position. Then there was the day I answered the phone and a woman in a ridiculously happy voice said, 'Hello, Mrs Scott, Jocelyn here from the RSPCA, how are you today?' I burst into tears and told Jocelyn that I was in a dreadful state. She listened to my plight and then said, 'Well, Mrs Scott, perhaps you'd like to help the RSPCA by buying some biros?' I bought the biros and it did make me feel better knowing that I was at least able to help an unhappy dog or cat.

I was angry too. I didn't intend to take it out on a complete stranger in our local shopping centre carpark but that's exactly what happened. I was coming back from the fruit and vegetable mart when I saw a chap standing between two cars. I looked at him and thought, 'Is he ...? My God, could he be ...? I don't believe this. He is, he's exposing himself!' I abandoned my shopping trolley, marched over to him and screamed, 'I've had a gutful! Do you understand me? I've had an absolute gutful of men and their dicks. I don't want to see it. They [referring to onlookers who had gathered] don't want to see it. No one wants to see it. Do you understand me? So for God's sake, put it away, keep it away and don't you EVER hang it out in public again!' And by the look on his face, I suspect he never did.

John, the eternal happy optimist, was the saddest I'd ever seen him. He looked terrible. He visited us all the time, and I mean *all the time*. As the kids correctly observed, 'We see more of Dad now that he doesn't live here than we ever saw him when he did.'

One of the worst consequences of John moving out was having to tell my mother the news; I dreaded making that call. She adored John. He was a brilliant son-in-law. All she had to do was ring and John would drop everything and race out to Greensborough to replace Mum's fire-alarm, or clean out her spouting, or climb up into the roof and check for rats. Mum also loved that we'd managed to hold a family together. According to Marg, there was NOTHING more important in life than that. I was sure she'd blame me for our demise.

I dialled her number. I braced myself for her disappointment and disapproval. I told her very briefly about the affair and she muttered something about men being stupid sometimes. And then she said, 'Oh Denise, I do love you, you know.' I hung up the phone and wept. The real reason I wept was because Mum didn't know the full story behind John's departure and I didn't want to tell her. Of course I didn't. What daughter wants to confess to her mother that she has contributed to a family breakdown? I preferred my mum to think it was all John's fault.

A year and a half earlier, John, the kids and I had moved into a small flat up the street while number 26 was being renovated. A team of like-minded, hippie-style, environmentally aware builders had set to work tearing down the back half of our house. Like many others of our generation, we were replacing it with a large open-plan living/dining area.

A quick word of warning: the open-plan dream seems like the most sensible thing in the world when your kids are young. It's only when they hit adolescence that you realise it's nuts because the LAST place an adolescent wants to be when they're hanging out with their friends, or even on their own for that matter, is in the same room as their parents. I know of a family who, after spending a fortune building an award-winning, architect-designed, open-plan living area was then forced to erect a series of unattractive, makeshift, plywood walls recreating the small rooms they had just torn down. The final effect was not dissimilar to a row of shantytown brothels in a Kalgoorlie street. This was all because their teenage kids needed privacy to pursue their Facebook and MySpace activities. But the issue of adolescents and their needs was still some way off for us so we proceeded in blissful ignorance.

During the reno period John was working flat-out. I wasn't working so I was landed with the responsibility of making all the tough decisions, like choosing the doorknobs, taps and light fittings. The renovations presented all the usual stresses such as the ceiling rose crashing to the floor a minute after we'd been standing there admiring it, the chimney coming close to collapse, and the shade of white turning out not to be the shade of white promised on the colour chart. But I guess it was the fact that I had an affair with the builder that really took our home reno nightmares to new heights. And I have to acknowledge that the builder being one of John's best friends at the time took these particular renovation stresses off the emotional Richter scale.

I had written about this entanglement on a piece of paper, trying to work through what I should do about it. I'd put the piece of paper in the pocket of my dressing gown – except that it wasn't just my dressing gown; John and I shared it. To this day, John remains wary of putting his hand in a dressing-gown pocket, scared of what life-changing item he may find.

This was big. This was momentous. This was a catastrophe. Uncertainty, broken hearts, shock, tears, guilt, anger, love, passion, pain and hurt – you name the emotion, we covered it; there was even an ulcer involved. With no one quite knowing what to do, the builder left the project a little earlier than expected and John and I moved back into number 26, which fortunately was close to completion, except for the bathroom.

While the kids excitedly explored their new bedrooms, John and I sat in the middle of the new open-plan living area looking like a couple of war-torn, shell-shocked refugees. The bay window, with its delicate leadlight glass, the highly polished golden Baltic pine floorboards and the steeple ceiling, featuring inlaid parquetry in the shape of a star, created an almost church-like sense of peace. But in reality we were in turmoil.

We attempted to get our lives back to normal. By 'normal' I mean John resumed his manic work schedule, driving big trucks under small bridges, and I went back to TV with a sad heart and no commitment to it and hey, I got the sack. It wasn't until I threw that piece of pig at John's head that we both snapped out of our emotional paralysis and took some action. We knew we couldn't go on living like this and that's when John moved out and we had a rest from each other.

While we lived apart we came to four conclusions: a) we were both miserable living together but we were even more miserable living apart; b) we both loved living in number 26; c) we both loved spending every single day with our children; and d) we'd both been stupid and cruel to each other and maybe, just maybe, with the help of some good counselling and Tony Delroy's midnight quiz, we might find our way back to loving each other again.

John moved back in.

Fourteen years later we have definitely managed to find our way back to love but unfortunately the bathroom remains unfinished.

CHAPTER 13

Giving up cigarettes

Sometimes, when my kids were little and gorgeous and happy and healthy and well-adjusted and John and I were getting on really well and we had our cosy house and ate good food and our extended families and friends were all going well and the unemployment rate was down and the economy was up, I would find myself lying in bed of a morning, thinking, 'What's the point? What's the point of getting up?' And then I would remember, 'Of course, a cigarette.' And immediately I had the will and the motivation to bounce out of bed and face a new day.

Of course, I gave up smoking about 23 kilograms ago now, but to this day there are times when I miss it because the truth is I loved smoking. I mean I LOVED it. I mean really LOVED it. Oh, this is when I gnash my teeth and lament that I'm not Tolstoy or Dostoyevsky or Nabokov, whose literary talents would have been up to the task of conveying the true depth, the intensity, the many layers of meaning to that word 'love' when it comes to describing my relationship with a Benson and Hedges 16 mg filter-tip smoke. I even loved the packaging, with its shiny gold surface, the stylish lettering and that flip-top lid.

I particularly loved the first cigarette of the day. I would get up early, make myself a strong coffee in the espresso pot and head outside to the backyard. And then I would light up and then I would inhale and then I would exhale and then I would feel happy. Yes, I would feel quite blissful – well, once I had stopped coughing I would feel blissful. Oh yes, I would cough, alright, because as well as being a smoker I am also an asthmatic. Have I already mentioned that? Either way, I never did like those two facts stated in the same sentence, especially by John who would occasionally attempt to say something like, 'Your breathing's bad today, Scotty. Do you think you should be smoking that cig …'

'Don't start, John, just don't start. You don't understand. This is the only thing I've got at the moment that is giving me any happiness, so please, I'm begging you, don't start.'

Ah yes, that first ciggie in the morning. There I would be, standing in the backyard wearing cousin Gavin's ugg boots and the threadbare terry-towelling dressing gown. I would have a cigarette in my left hand and a coffee in my right. As I smoked and sipped I would bask in the solitude and study the sky with its pale, early-morning light. I would observe the brightly coloured lorikeets that would be kicking up a storm in our orange flowering gumtree. (I assume the lorikeets still do this today but I wouldn't know. Since giving up smoking I've stopped going outside and taking any interest in nature.) Back in those heady, carefree, nicotine-fuelled days, at some point in this morning ritual I would place my coffee on the ground and from the right pocket of the dressing gown I would produce a Ventolin inhaler and have a couple of puffs. (I always wondered why no one had ever thought of combining a packet of cigarettes and a Ventolin inhaler in a nicely presented gift-pack. It would have been my ideal Christmas present.)

Often, it seemed to be at that exact moment – standing in the backyard with a cigarette in one hand and Ventolin puffer in the other – that I would look up and see my two little kids staring at me out of the glass-panelled door. Oh, what the hell were they doing awake? I would begin to frantically wave my arms in a desperate bid to mime a message that I would be much happier if they turned around and went back to bed. Didn't they understand that mothers needed a moment to themselves every now and again?

My mum had smoked like a chimney. Well, of course she did; she was a nurse. She worked at the geriatric hospital across the road from our house. In fact, it was the matron who first got Mum onto cigarettes – to keep her awake and help her relax during nightshift. Pretty soon all the nurses at the geriatric home became smokers. Years later, in the early '80s, when the Ash Wednesday bushfires occurred and all of Melbourne was covered in thick, choking smoke and visibility was nil and there were big flakes of ash floating through the air, I remember thinking, 'Wow, this is exactly what it used to look like in the staffroom at the Deloraine Nursing Home during their morning tea-break.' Eight nurses, all wearing Edna Everage glasses and stiff, white caps that sat precariously atop their Queen Elizabeth–inspired perms, would drink hot cups of tea, eat Savoy biscuits and cheese, and chat and smoke with gusto.

I was very familiar with this scene because when I had to stay home from school due to my severe asthma attacks I was allowed to hang out with Mum in the staffroom. I'd sit in the corner wheezing away as these vibrant women would be sucking the life out of an Albany cigarette and remarking, 'Gee Marg, Denise's asthma's bad today. What do you think's causing it?'

'I don't know.'

'Do you think it might be emotional?'

'Mmm, could be. She *is* one of those kids who seem to have an attack every time she gets excited.'

'Lucky she lives in Greensborough then. Excitement won't be too much of a problem here.'

And they would all laugh until one of them would have a coughing fit.

'Oh, here you go, June, have one of my Alpines. They're menthol-flavoured. They'll help your throat.'

Mum gave up smoking when she was in her seventies and had her third heart attack, which happened while she was in hospital recovering from her second. When it came my turn to give up smoking, I proved to be very good at it. In fact, I was so good at it that I think I gave up about seventeen times before I finally stopped for good.

A particularly memorable, I'm-going-to-give-up-smoking moment occurred one day when I had taken the kids out for a walk in their double pusher. We had gone to a very large park where I sat down to have a cigarette. I only had one match and as I lit it a sudden gust of wind immediately blew it out. Devastated, I walked around that park asking people, *imploring* people, for a match. No luck. I was just in the process of looking for two sticks to rub together when, in the distance, I spotted some workmen smoking. Oh, great and glorious, happy, happy day! They were sitting in a work area enclosed by a very tall cyclone fence. I yelled at them, 'Excuse me!' No response. I yelled louder, 'EXCUSE ME ...' Once more, no response; they were too far away to hear. So I parked the pusher and told Jordie and Bonnie not to move, 'Mummy will be back in a minute.' With that, I began to scale the cyclone fence. At the top I hurled myself over and landed with a thud on the other side. I walked over to the group of workmen and asked them for a light. They looked surprised to see me there, but kindly lit my cigarette. I stood awkwardly smoking while they continued chatting to one another. My kids sat in the pusher on the other side of the fence, looking perplexed.

As I took my last drag, I began to feel just a tad self-conscious that I was now going to have to turn around, walk back to the fence and climb it in order to get out. I proceeded to do so, trying to appear as casual and confident as possible which, considering I could feel the stare of the workmen's incredulous eyes on me from behind, and I could see my children's incredulous eyes on me from the front, wasn't easy. When I had climbed a little way up the fence one of the workmen came over and asked, 'Excuse me, but why don't you go out the gate?' He pointed to a spot nearby.

'Thank you,' I said as I climbed down and walked through the nearby gate that was indeed wide open. Later that day I announced that I was giving up cigarettes.

It's a well-known but rarely discussed fact that pretty soon after you announce you've given up smoking for good and everyone congratulates you and says things like, 'I really admire your courage and determination', you'll enter your secret smoking phase. This starts with picking up butts from the street and proceeds to emptying out your rubbish bin and muttering, 'Eureka!' when you come across a stinking, sodden, half-smoked cigarette that you'll pop in the oven to dry. Pretty soon you'll buy a packet, which you'll then keep hidden at the back of your underpants drawer, eagerly awaiting the moment your partner leaves for work so you can sneak around the side of the house and crouch down beside your big, open compost mound and proceed to light up. And it is usually at this very moment when you're about to have your first illicit puff that you'll hear a yell: 'Mum, where are you?'

I would then hear Bonnie ask Jordie, 'Have you seen Mum?' That's when I would hear their little footsteps pattering all around the house as they called out, 'Mum, Mum, where are you?' And next thing they'd be out in the backyard, 'MUM, MUM...' Oh Jesus Christ, they're getting closer. So I would panic and dive for cover, this time lying flat on the ground behind the compost heap, sucking furiously on a cigarette while my children became more and more distressed, wondering whether their mother had abandoned them. (This behaviour may seem cruel to some. But I argue that at the time it was necessary for my mental health.)

When John was home, my favourite secret smoking spot was behind a large tree in a nearby shopping centre carpark. This meant I was forever dashing down the street. 'Just going to get some milk, John.'

'But Scotty, we've got plenty.'

'Yes, but um ... um ... I might want to ... make custard.'

It was this secret activity that caused me to nearly have heart failure one night. At the time I was working on

Tonight Live. We'd finished our 'Clean Up Your Act' segment and during the ad break, just as I was leaving the studio floor, Steve said, 'Denise, why don't you stick around? I'd like you to come and sit on the couch with me and be involved in the next segment.' His mouth kept moving but I had stopped listening. I had stopped listening because I had gone into full-scale panic. I had gone into full-scale panic because a 'hidden camera' segment had recently been introduced to the show. This involved secretly filming celebrities, or even familiar cast and crew members, doing something like an illegal carpark, showing it to the national audience and making lots of jokes at their expense. I was a regular on the show and hence I became convinced that I'd been filmed smoking behind the tree in the carpark or worse ... oh, Jesus Christ no. Oh God, what if they'd used a long range lens and ...? Oh no ... no. I would never recover from the shame.

We were nearly at the end of the ad break. I looked at Steve Vizard and said, 'If you're about to show hidden camera footage of me lying down behind my compost heap smoking while my children run around crying and searching for me, I'll walk off the set. I will, Steve.'

He just looked at me. By now we were back on air. He went on to introduce some relatively unknown mother who had a new book out on parenting, and Steve thought it would work better to have me there as part of the interview.

I finally stopped smoking when I was about forty-two. It was post-renovations and my smoking had skyrocketed. Weirdly enough, I don't remember the exact year let alone the date I said goodbye forever to my beloved friends, Benson and Hedges. Without doubt I gave up because of John's mum, Nan.

Nan was (and my use of past tense should give you a hint as to how and why Nan helped me to give up) a really good-looking woman. She had a strong jawline and really good cheekbones, and she'd been a fit and healthy mother of five who spent her days cooking fabulous food, playing tennis and doing lots of housework. During the 1960s, housework was made more bearable for Nan by Rothmans cigarettes. She would have one burning in an ashtray in every room in the house. This way she could simply move from room to room and not have to take a cigarette with her. Of course, these were the days when smoking didn't give you cancer, it gave you satisfaction, and women especially loved its liberating quality.

Nan had stopped smoking in her early fifties, before I even met her. She shared great 'giving up' stories with me: the usual fishing butts out of the bin, or finding a cigarette in her husband's dinner suit that he hadn't worn for years, or coming across the occasional butt on the street when out shopping which, hey, all us smokers have done at one time or another but we're not usually dressed in an exquisitely tailored outfit from Georges as Nan would always be. Nan never, ever, not once, suggested I give up smoking. She didn't have to. She would simply walk around her beautiful, tastefully furnished home, her oxygen cylinder on its trolley wheeling along beside her, plastic tubes in each of her nostrils, and the constant sucking sound of air being inhaled. Amazingly, she still managed to look glamorous and dignified. But she would have to watch as her husband, children and grandchildren headed off down the beach, which was only a minute from her house, but you had to descend a steep hill and of course climb back up it at the end of your swim.

I felt lousy that people who started smoking in the 1940s, '50s, even '60s, following in the footsteps of their glamorous Hollywood movie stars, didn't know that they would have to pay such a price for their pleasure. But because of Nan I *did* know, without a doubt, the price you can pay. And so I gave up.

I didn't have any work at the time, which was handy because I always used to have a smoke before I went on stage to calm my nerves, and I always had one when I came off stage to recover. I always had a cigarette before I started writing, and when I got to a tricky spot I would go outside and have a cigarette and contemplate the problem, and then after I had come back inside and solved the problem, I would go back outside and have a cigarette to celebrate. You get the picture.

I went cold turkey and it was excruciating. I cried a lot. My grief was profound. I grieved so badly that one night when John was later than ever arriving home, I convinced myself that he may have been killed in a car accident. I went on to think, 'That means I'll be smoking again; I mean, no one would blame me under the circumstances, being a grieving widow and all.'

Just as I was figuring out how and where I could get some ciggies at that time of night, what do you know? John walked in the door. 'Hi Scotty.' My face fell. 'Scotty, what's the matter?'

'You're alive.'

'Of course I am. You seem so disappointed.'

I knew it would be pointless trying to explain my feelings to a man who'd never smoked cigarettes in his life.

To help me cope with nicotine withdrawals, I decided to keep myself busy by concentrating on a craft project. I've always loved doing crafty things like knitting and embroidery, patchwork and mosaic. But during the smoking-withdrawal period, I decided to decoupage all six of our kitchen chairs. For those of you not familiar with decoupage, it's the art of cutting out pictures and sticking them onto things. In kindergarten we used to call it cut and paste. And so I cleared a space in our shed and every day I would disappear in there. Away I went, sanding, stripping, painting, gluing, varnishing; sanding, stripping, painting, gluing, varnishing; sanding, stripping, painting, gluing, varnishing; sanding, stripping, painting, gluing, varnishing until finally, two months later, I emerged with six individually themed, decoupaged kitchen chairs and no more nicotine cravings.

About a week after completing this project, I was sitting at the kitchen table on one of the chairs (possibly the pink one featuring the fish and palm-tree theme) reading the *Herald Sun*. They'd published a special report on the latest medical research involving visual artists, and guess what? It turns out that stripping, painting, varnishing and gluing emit dangerous toxic chemicals that cause cancer. Well, isn't that just great. I could clearly see myself in the hospital, lying in the oxygen tent, gasping my last breaths. And when the time came for them to pull the sheet over my head, sympathetic people would tactfully whisper to John and the kids, 'So, was it the cigarettes that killed her?'

'No,' they'd reply, 'it was her kitchen chairs.'

CHAPTER 14

Back to the womb

n the late 1990s I appeared on an ABC TV show called *The Smallest Room in the House*. Each week, one comedian would perform a half-hour autobiographical story to a small studio audience. It was then some weeks before it went to air. I decided my monologue was going to be about my abnormal womb. I admit that it doesn't immediately strike one as a potentially funny or, for that matter, remotely interesting topic. But I didn't want to tell a story on national TV that involved friends or family. Put it this way, I thought it better to talk about my womb than the home renovations.

If I hadn't gone for a pap smear on that particular day all those years earlier, it's quite possible that I could have gone through life never knowing that I had a bicornuate uterus. I was twenty-six at the time, living in Albury, and fully immersed in my relationship with John. All the girls in town were racing off to have pap smears because Joy, a popular local barmaid, had recently had one and been diagnosed with cervical cancer.

So there I was, lying on the bed at the doctor's, and he was just about to insert the speculum when I was overcome with more than the usual sense of panic one experiences when a stranger is about to shove a cold, metal paddle up your vagina. I said, 'Um, look, just before you do that, I'm a bit overdue with my period.'

'How overdue?'

'Oh, about six or seven ... weeks. And I've been feeling a bit nauseous and gee, my breasts have been tender.'

'You could be pregnant.'

'What?'

'You could be pregnant.'

'How?'

'Well, sex is the usual cause.'

'No, I mean how could I be pregnant when I've got an IUD in?'

The doctor looked serious. 'In that case it could be ectopic.'

'What?'

'Ectopic. The pregnancy's in your fallopian tube.'

'Where?'

'Your fallopian tube. You'll have to go to hospital immediately. They'll do a laparoscopy ...'

'A what?'

'A laparoscopy. They put you under, have a look around and if it's ectopic, they'll cut it out. Then again, it could be a cyst. Then again, it could be a normal pregnancy. Then again ... it could be anything.'

'Well, I don't think it's a lounge suite.'

No, I didn't really say that. Of course I didn't. I said nothing and left the doctor's.

John was away at the time so I went to the hospital alone. I was washed down, gowned up and knocked out. I regained consciousness a couple of hours later. I hadn't been cut open so I knew it wasn't an ectopic pregnancy or a cyst.

'It was a normal pregnancy,' said the specialist.

My eyes lit up. 'So I'm pregnant?'

'No, we aborted you.'

To be fair, maybe this specialist did offer a reasonable explanation for this course of action but if he did I certainly didn't hear it. Perhaps I was too busy reeling.

'You probably would have lost it anyway. You see, it appears you may have what seems like an abnormal womb. You should have it X-rayed.'

So, I'd been aborted without permission and told I've got a weird womb, the implication being that I may never have children. Gee, this day had certainly taken a different direction from my initial plan of going to the doctor's, then the laundromat, then the coffee-shop for lunch, and then home to watch some telly.

The following night I went to Maudie's Wine Bar in downtown Dean Street. Joy, the popular barmaid, was working behind the bar. She poured each of us a whisky, leant across the bar and said, 'Well, Scotty, you've got a fucked fanny and I've got cancer of the cunt. Cheers.'

It was Joy's famous line that, fourteen years later, was causing me some nightmares. I had included it in my monologue for *The Smallest Room in the House*. I'd done so because I loved its shocking poignancy. Realising that my appreciation of Joy's words might not be shared by all, I'd written the piece so that they could easily be edited out before going to air.

The show's producers certainly appreciated the worth of such a quote and fought hard to retain it. And so it was with much excitement that one of the producers, Hugh, rang me and excitedly announced, 'Congratulations Scotty, you're going to be the first person on national TV to say fuck and cunt in the same sentence!'

In that split second my mother's face loomed. Oh, how it loomed. It wasn't a happy face. It was a face of utter disapproval. And since Dad had died, Mum didn't have Russ to reassure her, 'Oh, don't worry, Marg. She's a good kid. Just a bit crazy, that's all.' I know it's utterly pathetic to care that much about your mother's approval when you're a grown-up with a couple of kids yourself, and besides, what on earth had I been expecting? Sure, it stands to reason that Mr and Mrs Hillary were beside themselves when Edmund climbed Mt Everest; and Mr and Mrs Curie swelled with pride over Marie's contribution to world health; but realistically, how easy would it be for any mother, let alone one born in 1924 into a very strict, straight, small-town Catholic family, to beam with pride that her daughter was making history by saying *those* words on TV – the very words that as a child my mother told me you would be arrested and sent to jail for daring to utter.

The week before the show went to air Mum had a major heart attack and was rushed to hospital in an ambulance. She was making a good recovery when she had another heart attack. We raced to her bedside, thinking that this could well be it. It's a terrible admission, but as we drove to the hospital in solemn silence, I thought to myself, 'If Mum does die, at least she won't see me swear on the telly,' and I did feel quite a sense of relief.

But Mum fully recovered and was out of hospital the night the show was screened. Over the following couple of days I received many positive phone calls and great feedback about the show. It was favourably reviewed in the papers with words like 'pathos', 'laughter', and 'tears' appearing in the same sentence. In fact, I probably got more congratulatory feedback about that gig than any other I'd done; but as the days went by and there was no phone call from my mum, I felt sicker and sicker. I decided I would have to confront this stand-off. I rang her.

She was steely cold. I took a deep breath and said, 'So, did you see the show the other night?'

There was silence. I waited for the bomb to drop and when it did, even I was shocked by its ferocity. 'Yes, I saw the show and I hated it,' she said.

I'd never heard Mum use the word 'hate' with such sincerity. My guts heaved. Immediately, I wanted to take refuge under my doona and sob. I mumbled something about the swearing as I was sure it would have been the cause of Mum's angst. But no, she didn't care about that. I was stunned and humbled to discover that somehow Mum thought the show was about her, believing that she'd been the cause of my weird womb. She said, 'There are some things that should never be discussed in public and that's one of them.' Her sense of humiliation could not have been greater.

The next week I took the kids to visit Mum. Things were still awkward between us. We were having a cup of tea when she stood up to get something from the top of the fridge. It was a letter. She put it down in front of me on the kitchen table. It was addressed to her. As is often the case with Mum, she offered no explanation whatsoever. It sat there in front of me until I gathered from the deafening silence that Mum wanted me to read it. I turned over the envelope, which was already open, and took out the letter.

It was from an old war buddy, a woman Mum had nursed with at the Heidelberg Repat Hospital during the Second World War. She now lived in Queensland and had seen me performing the womb story on the ABC. She'd loved it. She thought it was a wonderful piece of writing and such a moving story and she could only guess at 'how proud you must be, Margaret, seeing your daughter doing such a wonderful job on the television.'

I put the letter back in the envelope, Mum put it back on top of the fridge and we never referred to it again.

CHAPTER 15

Some important advice re: the parenting of adolescents that you may never hear anywhere else

 ne day, a few years back, I was chatting with actress Sigrid Thornton while we were hanging about on the set of the TV series, *SeaChange*. (If this sounds like I'm name-dropping then good, I have achieved my goal.)

Alright, let's be honest here. I had a walk-on guest role as a vet in one of Sigrid's court cases. I had one line of dialogue, of which I have absolutely no memory. What I do vividly recall was the wardrobe lady coming into my dressing room and handing me a pair of size 22 pants. She explained apologetically, 'They were all I could find. Pop them on, see how you go and I'll alter them.' I put them on and immediately went into an Oh–God–kill–me–now slump. They fitted me perfectly.

It was while I was wearing these size 22, morale-boosting trousers that I got chatting to the perfect, beautiful both within and without, ridiculously young-looking Sigrid. We were discussing our adolescent kids and she said something I've never forgotten.

'Look,' she said, 'at the end of the day, you just want them to come home alive, don't you?'

I grabbed that quote and often of a night I would hang onto it like grim death as I lay in bed wondering, 'Where are they? Who are they with? What are they doing? Are they drinking? Are they smoking? Should I have a talk to them about contraception or just tell them not to have sex until they're at least thirty? Should we go looking for them? Should I try their mobile again? What if Bonnie's been taken somewhere against her will? What if Jordie gets bashed because he's a bit tubby and not very good at basketball? Should I ring another parent and see if they know anything? Is it too soon to ring the police? Should I tell them I found a little chillum and lighter hidden in one of Bonnie's Doc Marten boots or should I just ignore it? Oh God Almighty, help me ...' And that's when I would remember Sigrid's quote and I'd forget all my other concerns and focus on praying, willing them to come home alive. Anything else John and I would cope with, if they just managed to get home in one piece.

It's not the easiest of times for adolescent kids either. They squirm inside their own bodies which are always too fat or too skinny or too tall or too short, and they have big ears that stick out from tiny heads, or have big heads that sit on top of scrawny bodies. And they usually smell, especially boys. They stink. If you don't believe me, just pay a visit to any fourteen-year-old boy's bedroom. It's like finding yourself inside a giant, sweaty, putrid running shoe that has been worn by someone with a foot odour problem on a forty-degree day. Truth, as they say, can be a harsh thing.

And for those wondering why the ice-caps are melting and the polar bear faces extinction, you need look no further than an adolescent boy's overzealous use of underarm deodorant, which they spray all over their body about sixteen times a day. At first it may seem that they're trying to compensate for their smell but it's more likely a much more primitive instinct. As the TV ads tell you, if you're a young guy and you walk past a gorgeous, tall, leggy woman and she gets a whiff of your deodorant, she will immediately go into a trance-like state, follow and attempt to kiss you; she can't help herself. The truth is, if you do follow a young man who has just covered himself in half a can of such a substance, you're more likely to start wheezing and have an asthma attack.

Meanwhile, adolescent girls are either fully developed with beautiful, sexy breasts and curvy hips and look about twenty-eight years old or else they're tiny, with no breasts, and look about six. Then there's the poor, fat friend, who from behind could be mistaken for a 45-year-old.

Bonnie was recently recalling her adolescence. 'Mum, remember where you were when I told you I'd got my first period?'

I thought for a moment and replied as honestly as I could, 'No.'

'I'm not surprised,' she said. 'You were pissed and lying in the hammock and didn't seem interested at all.'

'Oh, really? I am sorry about that.'

John, on the other hand, lost his mind about the news and, much to Bonnie's dismay, went and bought a bottle of champagne; worse still, he gathered the family together, poured everyone a glass and proposed a toast: 'To Bonnie. Congratulations on becoming a woman. Cheers.'

It's important that adolescents have somewhere to go to get away from adults. Since we now had an open-plan living area, Jordie and Bonnie would seek refuge in their childhood cubby house. John had built it himself. It was made entirely of wood that John got for free after the local council replaced the playground equipment in a nearby park. He was thrilled. 'I'll be able to build the kids an authentic log cabin.'

John sawed and hammered and drilled, creating a real little Hansel and Gretel cottage. The fact that, upon completion of the cubby, we discovered the reason the wood had been removed from public playgrounds was that it had been treated with arsenic did not deter John. 'Well, it's not as if the kids are going to lick the cubby walls, are they?'

The kids hardly ever played in it. This wasn't to do with the arsenic because, being responsible parents, we never shared this detail; it would only have upset them. They claimed it was a bit spooky. Whatever. But come those adolescent years, the cubby finally came into its own.

One Friday night I arrived home at about 11.30 pm after performing in a theatre production called *Mum's the Word*. We were playing to packed houses eight times a week. Most of the audience were women, and in an ironic twist that I hope will soon become evident, it was a play about the ups and downs of motherhood. Bonnie was snuggled on the couch watching TV and John and I were seated at the kitchen table having a glass of wine. Jordie and four friends (all around thirteen years old) were in the cubby.

At about 11.35 pm there was a knock at the front door. When I answered I was surprised to see two uniformed police officers standing outside. 'Excuse me, sorry to trouble you, but do you currently have a group of young boys on this property?' Oh dear.

'Yes,' I gulped.

They explained that earlier that evening they'd received a call from a motorist who'd complained that, when driving past our house, he had been assaulted by a group of young boys, who'd thrown rolled-up bits of wet toilet paper at his car. One of the policemen added that he had recently attended a fatal accident. Two young boys standing on an overpass that spanned a major freeway nearby had been throwing rocks at cars speeding along the road beneath them. One went through a windscreen, hitting the driver and consequently killing him. These 'bored' adolescents were now facing manslaughter charges. 'Oh, I see,' I said. This same earnest and caring policeman then asked if it would be alright 'if I had a talk to the young gentlemen concerned'.

John, Bonnie and I stood on the back porch and watched wide-eyed as the policemen, with guns in their holsters and crackling voices emanating from their walkie-talkies, walked across our backyard towards the cubby. I could just discern the flickering of pale candlelight in the small gaps between the toxic logs. I could hear the hushed whispering and stifled laughter coming from within. The concerned officers stood outside the tiny doorway. One of them cleared his throat.

'Police here.'

Shocked silence from within the cubby. 'Police here, we're coming in.' And so these two policemen, bent over double, walked through the tiny doorway into the cubby. We heard their stern voices and the polite replies of the young offenders. Minutes later the officers re-emerged, stood back upright, dusted themselves down and retraced their steps across the yard.

To research this story, I set off late one afternoon,

travelled across our hallway and asked Jordie how he'd felt when the police appeared in the cubby all those years ago.

'Ma, we shat ourselves.'

'I see. And look, just out of interest, what were you guys doing in the cubby that night?'

'I can't tell you that, Ma.'

I learnt something new about Jordie that day. I learnt that if ever he was captured for being a spy, his torturers would only have to say, 'Oh go on, tell us …'

'Ma, the idea was that we'd all pitch in and bring whatever we could. Someone brought a cigar, someone else a packet of cigarettes, another kid had some of his dad's porn magazines, and there was the vodka that had been taken from a kitchen cupboard and poured into pop-top juice bottles. And then there was the weed …'

'Weed? You were thirteen years old and smoking weed in the cubby when the police arrived?'

'Yeah.'

Oh dear. Maybe they had licked the walls after all.

It is extremely rare for me to make a straight-out, black and white statement; it's generally not my style. It is even rarer for me to make a black and white statement regarding a parenting issue. But if there is one thing I do know after all these years it is this: NEVER, EVER LET YOUR CHILD CONVINCE YOU TO HAVE A FIFTEENTH BIRTHDAY PARTY. DON'T ASK WHY, JUST TRUST ME ON THIS.

They are a nightmare. They are never worth it. I can't believe that it's not a universally accepted practice to never allow your child to convince you to let them have a fifteenth birthday party. Do I have to repeat myself or is the message clear that you should never, ever allow your child to convince you to let them have a fifteenth birthday party?

The reason I say with such certainty that you must NEVER, EVER LET YOUR CHILD CONVINCE YOU TO HAVE A FIFTEENTH BIRTHDAY PARTY is that I see this event as the point when we at number 26 officially said farewell to the age of innocence once and for all, and the sleepless nights worrying about our kids began in earnest.

Of course, there are those smug, neat-as-a-pin, hokey-pokey puppy parents who are right now sitting back thinking to themselves, 'But the fifteenth celebration we had for our Holly was delightful! Six girls set up camp in the lounge room and had a movie marathon of their favourite musicals. They started with *Grease* followed by *The Sound of Music* and went crazy with their all-time favourite, *Chicago*. Holly had all the lyrics typed up and they sang and danced along. We even had a special tap-dancing board on the floor because of course most of them had learnt to tap at their music theatre class. It was an absolute hoot! And they all got up the next morning and we had pancakes and maple syrup and hot chocolate together, and then those girls, would you believe, cleaned up the kitchen, cleared away the bedding from the lounge, and honestly, you wouldn't ever have known they'd been there.'

Yeah, well, good for you Mr and Mrs Holly but believe me, you are in the minority and for those like me who reside with the majority of struggling parents: just in case you haven't quite grasped my point, I'll say it one more time: NEVER, EVER LET YOUR CHILD CONVINCE YOU TO HAVE A FIFTEENTH BIRTHDAY PARTY.

Of course John and I had said to Jordie, 'There is to be no alcohol, do you understand?' And he'd said, 'Yes.' And we'd believed him. Yes, alright, we should have been suspicious when that afternoon he seemed unduly preoccupied with setting up eskies and kept asking John, 'Could you buy me some ice, Dad?'

'We don't need to. We've got a couple of trays in the freezer.'

'That won't be enough, Dad.'

And to think I just laughed and quietly muttered to John, 'Since when have kids cared about how chilled their lemonade is?'

The party kicked off at 7 pm. By 7.30 about seventy kids had arrived, most of them wearing backpacks that clinked, and you know what an adolescent wearing a clinking backpack means? Vomit, and plenty of it. According to all reports, the first sign of trouble was when a kid threw one of my homemade sausage rolls at

173

the back of another kid's neck, which in turn caused him to hurl the first vomit. (I apologise to those repulsed by the word vomit, and I must give warning that I'll be using it a lot more before I'm through telling this coming-of-age tale.)

By 9 pm, John – happy, effusive John who truly is in competition with the Dalai Lama when it comes to seeing the positive side of everything – officially declared the situation to be a 'state of emergency'. He called his brother Peter, who raced over immediately. The three of us and a couple of lovely, young Christian-type girls, who would have fitted in perfectly at Holly's musical marathon, spread out across the yard armed with wet towels, face-washers, mops and buckets. We responded to cries of, 'Help, over here! Veronica's started spewin'.'

'Oh my God, Katie's spewin' now …'

'Denise, come quick, it's Luke, Anna and Jane; they're all spewin' at once …'

'Now Tim's started spewin'…'

'But Tim hasn't had a drink…'

'No, but he's spewin' cos he saw Katie spewin' and that made him spew.'

At one point I found myself standing in the kitchen, staring out the window trying to absorb the spectacle in our backyard. I can only liken it to a surreal scene out of a Fellini movie in which everything seems to move in slow motion. The fairy-lights that John had hung around the birch tree and the alder, and the multicoloured lights that were strung over the clothesline sparkled and illuminated the pale young faces as their mouths slowly parted, revealing the dazzling glint of the obligatory braces that their parents had taken out a second mortgage to provide. Their heads tilted back as they poured the cheap Mississippi Moonshine whisky straight from the bottle into their mouths. Then, after taking a deep drag on a Holiday cigarette, suddenly their faces contorted as they slowly leaned forward and hurled forth a combination of alcohol, homemade sausage rolls and mini-pizzas, which cascaded like a flowing fountain from their mouths into our backyard, which now resembled a multicoloured carpet of regurgitated food and drink. Adding to the atmosphere was Rage Against the Machine's famous track, 'Killing in the Name of' which was playing at full volume. For those unfamiliar with the song, the lyrics go something like: 'Fuck you, I won't do what you tell me, fuck you, I won't do what you tell me, fuck you, I won't do what you tell me ...' et cetera – although at one stage the words do change when the lead singer desperately screams, 'Crazy motherfucker!' I wondered if Holly and her friends had ever sung along to that one.

It was at this point that I saw a kid eating one of my sausage rolls. I was pretty certain of this tasty little parcel's fate, and I remembered all the time and effort I'd put into baking them. That's when I snapped. I yelled at a guy standing next to the sound system, 'Turn the music off!' He just looked at me. 'Yes you, you with the hat and

the longneck in your hand, TURN THE MUSIC OFF!'
I walked towards him. 'TURN IT OFF NOW.' He
turned off the music. I marched outside and stood in the
middle of the yard and I yelled, 'I am so disappointed in
all of you. John and I have put a lot of time into this
party and you ...' A kid near me vomited. 'Oh, stop your
vomiting!'

He looked at me with genuine remorse and said,
'Sorry, Miss.'

I continued with my speech that, to my surprise and
disappointment, has never made it into one of those Great
Speeches in History books. 'We said there was to be no
alcohol and that means there is to be no alcohol drunk at
this party. Do you understand?'

'I saw you drinking, Miss.'

'YES, AND I'M IN MY FORTIES AND IT'S MY
SON'S PARTY AND I WAS THE ONE WHO GAVE
BIRTH TO HIM AND THERE'S GOT TO BE
SOME REWARD FOR GOING THROUGH THAT.
Alright, I am now going to come around and confiscate
all the remaining alcohol. If you come and see me before
you leave I shall return it to you. Do you understand
me?'

'Yes, Miss.'

Around this time a taxi arrived for a group of kids. I
went and found them. They were gathered around the
couch in our lounge room. As they stood up to leave,
they revealed a large girl who appeared to be

unconscious on the couch. For the sake of this girl's dignity, let's call her Alicia. As her friends headed outside to the cab, they explained in a most concerned way that they thought Alicia could be quite ill as she was a serious asthmatic and her breathing sounded terrible. They had promised Alicia's parents they would all go home together but 'we couldn't really get her to wake up ... so ... anyway, thanks for having us. And yeah, maybe you should take Alicia to, like, hospital or something cos, like, we think she might kind of, like ... maybe even die ...'

I managed to get Alicia's parents' phone number out of one of her caring friends before they sped away in the cab. Meanwhile, John and Peter had rolled her off the couch, dragged her down the hallway and got her sitting up on a chair on the front porch.

'Hello, is that Alicia's mother? Look, this is Denise Scott here, Jordie's mother. Yes, that's right, Alicia is here but, well, look, we're just a bit concerned, um, well, it appears she may be in a little bit of an alcoholic coma ...'

Meeting Alicia's horrified parents was one of the lower points of my life and, as John helped them drag Alicia's once-more comatose body into the back seat of their car, I recalled Sigrid Thornton's quote and I implored God to make Alicia live, which I'm happy to report, she did. Before driving away, Alicia's mother glared at me out of her car window and said, 'We thought there was to be no alcohol at this party.'

'So did we,' was all I could feebly mutter.

The last guest to leave was Jordie's music buddy, Simon. To get home, he only had to walk around the corner. 'Thanks for the party, Denise.'

'That's okay, Simon. Oh, and here, I've got your bottle of vodka, you can take it with you.'

'Why don't you keep it? You look as though you could use it more than me.'

There are good ways to handle the topic of sex with adolescents and there are not-so-good ways. The following is an example of a not-so-good way.

It happened one night while we were sitting at the kitchen table eating dinner. I said, 'John and I were talking last night, and we think we should have a discussion with you about sex.'

Bonnie screamed, 'Mum, that's gross!'

'It may well be, Bonnie, but we feel like we've been really irresponsible and we should be talking to you about these things.'

Jordie had slumped, his head in his hands. 'Mum, I'm sorry but this is ridiculous. I'm sixteen years old.'

'Yes, I know that, Jordie but, you know, there's things like ... well, like safe sex.'

Bonnie rolled her eyes. 'Mum, don't worry, we know about safe sex.'

I tried to sound confident. 'You may well know all about it, but your father and I are worried because the latest research says that kids your age aren't using condoms and we just want to make sure that you do.'

'Mum, you don't have to tell us this.'

'Well, I think we do have to tell you about safe sex, and while I'm on the topic I am going to say something, and it's probably going to gross you out, but I would feel I hadn't done my job as a parent if I didn't mention it. This research also said that, because of all this safe sex business, young girls are now being pressured to give guys blow jobs. It doesn't even have to be a special occasion apparently, it's just, "Hi, how are you?" and down they go.'

'Mum, that's disgusting.'

'Yeah, well, facts aren't always pretty, Bonn. I guess I just want you both to know that doing that sort of thing, well, it's not … you know … it's not normal. I mean, I'm not saying it's weird. I mean, there's plenty of people who enjoy it, although I've never understood it myself …'

'Oh Mum, *please* … that's repulsive!'

'All I'm saying, Bonnie, is that you shouldn't feel pressured to do anything you don't want to do. Okay?'

'Alright, Mum, whatever. Can we just, please, go now?'

John furrowed his brow as he tends to do when he wants to look serious, except that because he has no eyebrows he looks more like a mad professor in a cartoon show. 'Yes, but before you both go, what Scotty and I are really concerned about is safe sex and we just want to make sure that you use condoms because of … you know, unwanted pregnancies and the incidence of HIV is …'

'Dad, we know all this stuff.'

'Alright, Jordie. But tell me this: would you go into a chemist and buy a packet of condoms?'

'Dad, you can't ask Jordie that.'

'Why not, Bonnie? I'm his father.'

'Because it's embarrassing and it's none of your business, Dad.'

'Yeah, John, I agree with Bonnie. It is none of your business.'

'Will you shut up, Scotty? I'm trying to make a point.'

'There's no need to tell me to shut up, John.'

'Yes there is, Scotty. You interrupted me.'

'Well, for God's sake, just get on with it and make your point.'

'Alright then, I will. I think Jordie is the type of kid who would be too embarrassed to go into a chemist or a supermarket and buy condoms.'

'Oh, fuck off, Dad ...'

'Jordie, don't get upset, hear me out ...'

'Well, just hurry up and get to the point, John.'

'Alright, Scotty, I'm trying to. Okay, so ... what we've decided to do is we're going to put a box of condoms in the laundry cupboard. That way, they will be there for you to use when you need them.'

'Dad, this is crazy. We can look after ourselves.'

'That's fine, Jordie, I'm pleased to hear it. All I'm saying is there will be a box of communal condoms in the laundry cupboard. And I want to assure you that we will not count how many are in the box.'

'*You* mightn't, Dad, but as if Mum won't.'

'Good point, Bonnie, but I promise, I absolutely swear to God, that I will never, ever count how many condoms are in the box.'

John then made the following announcement: 'Unfortunately I didn't have enough time to go to the chemist today and buy a new box of condoms, so until I get the chance, I am going to go to our bedroom and get the box your mother and I use ... '

Bonnie's hand went to her mouth, 'Dad, that's making me feel sick.'

'... and I am going to put that box in the cupboard, just for now.'

At this point John arose from the table in a suitably serious and considered manner. He proceeded down the hall to our bedroom and returned carrying the box of condoms in both hands, holding it in front of his chest as one might a royal crown. Slowly and deliberately he marched across the kitchen, allowing time for us to reflect upon this important rite of passage. He disappeared into the laundry but within seconds had about-faced and was retracing his steps, still in slow-march mode, back across the kitchen, heading towards our bedroom. The box of condoms was still in his hand.

Without looking in our direction, he simply said, 'They're out of date.'

CHAPTER 16

Roxy Girl: a love story

ne of the best things about having little kids is the unconditional love they give you. When this same bundle of joy hits adolescence, you're lucky to get so much as a grunt when you dare to ask a hideously personal question such as, 'How was school?' And the only look you're ever likely to score is one that strongly indicates you are a total embarrassment to humankind. This leaves a big, dry well in a parent's heart; you long to be needed again by a little, fully dependent being who will adore you and give you their full devotion in return. That's why John and I did what lots of parents do in such circumstances – we got our first dog.

Raffi was, and for that matter still is, a mix of tiny terrier-type dogs, a little Hairy Maclary scruff-bucket who is equally hairy at both ends; so much so that patting him can be quite unnerving as you're never quite sure which end is which.

Then I bought another dog.

It happened one ordinary day when I'd headed off to the plaza with the ordinary expectation of buying some ordinary food for an ordinary dinner when lo and behold, something extraordinary happened. For the first time in my life I experienced the phenomenon of love at first sight, something I was not expecting to happen to me, especially at the plaza. I was in the pet shop. I don't even know why I went in there; it wasn't a usual haunt of mine. But in I went and there she was, Roxy Girl. She was a tiny, milk chocolate–coloured staffy/Jack Russell/ blue heeler cross. Our eyes met across a crowded cage and I was gone, hopelessly and utterly head–over–heels in love. I paid the sales girl $275 and arrived home with no food for dinner and a new member of the family.

Without doubt, I believe my deep connection with Roxy can be directly linked to a childhood trauma. When I was about eight years old my dad, Russ, took me to one of his footy mate's homes. I remember walking down their long driveway, which was lined with pine trees, holding my dad's hand because I found it a bit spooky. We went around to the back of the house and into an old shed. Lying in a darkened corner was a black labrador. She looked bushed and no wonder because when I got closer I saw the nine babies who were fighting to get some milk. My dad asked me to pick out a puppy that I would be able to take home in a couple of weeks. I picked out the only brown one in the litter. I called him Prince and I loved him. I wrote my first limerick in his honour and I've never forgotten it. As Tony Bennett would say, 'It goes a little something like this:'

> There once was a dog called Prince
> Who one day got into the mince
> Prince got a spank
> Off his master called Frank
> And he's never been near it since.

Thank you very much, ladies and gentleman, thank you kindly.

Now, you have to realise that this was in the days when people didn't have fences or gates, and dog leads were unheard of. And if your dog did a poo in the street, you would have been considered completely insane to pick it up and take it home with you in a plastic bag. In fact, come to think of it, in those days, there *were* no plastic bags. Thus Prince would follow me to school and I would have to drag him home by his collar and tell him to 'Stay, Prince. Stay.' And then I'd head back to school and five minutes later, there Prince would be, running amok in the classroom again. On Sundays when my mum, sister and I would be kneeling down in St Mary's church, our heads lowered and our eyes closed, saying the Mass, suddenly Prince would appear, jumping up onto the seat in front of us, enthusiastically licking our faces. Mum would keep her head bowed and whisper, 'Just pretend we don't know him.'

Prince would bite the pan man, usually while he was walking down our driveway balancing the Scott family waste products on his left shoulder. But it was when Mum opened the back door three mornings in a row to find Prince proudly sitting there with a neighbour's chook hanging limp in his mouth that it was decided something had to be done.

One afternoon I arrived home from school and there was no Prince. Mum was standing with her back to me, apparently looking for something in the fridge. 'Hey Mum, do you know where Prince is? I can't find him.'

'Oh, your father took him to the vet's and had him put down. Oh darn, there's no milk, I was going to make a tapioca pudding for tea.'

At number 26, everyone was very excited about Roxy's arrival – well, except for Raffi. Understandably, he was extremely put out and walked out the back door in a dramatic huff, refusing to come back inside.

Within days Raffi and Roxy were playing together and all was well with the world. I was crazy about Roxy. She followed me everywhere and loved being cuddled. She would sit at my feet with her head in my lap and gaze up at me with her George Clooney eyes. I guess what I'm trying to say is they were eyes you could drown in. Raffi was much more independent. He didn't seem to want cuddles and when we went to the park he would head off on his own, like an impatient cranky grandpa, while Roxy Girl played nonstop with me, catching the ball that I managed to throw a most pathetically short distance. And as I walked along the street with the two of them on leads, Roxy Girl would elicit involuntary 'Oohs' and 'Aaahs' from total strangers, who couldn't help but stop and pat her. Poor Raffi; he must have felt like the plain, daggy sibling who has a stunning, vivacious sister everyone raves about.

Anyone who is a dog person will have already picked up that this was not a good state of affairs; but let's just say that when it came to animals John and I were no Steve and Terri Irwin so we continued to live in blissful ignorance of the impending tragedy that appeared to be written in the stars, as they say.

About a year after Roxy Girl came to live with us she attacked Raffi. I was the only human home at the time. I had never seen a full-on dog attack and here it was, happening in my very own hallway. For those who haven't seen such a thing, you can imagine no other outcome but death for the poor 'loser'. As Roxy locked her jaw around Raffi's little throat and proceeded to tear him limb from limb, I did everything RSPCA president Hugh Wirth, who I listened to religiously on radio, had said not to do. I screamed. I screamed and screamed and screamed as though I was the one being murdered. Luckily I wasn't, as not one of my neighbours came to check on me. For days after, my throat felt shredded and my voice was rough and raspy. I also ignored Hugh Wirth's stern words advising that one must never try to intervene. I desperately dived in to the action and attempted to separate the dogs. I was sobbing and begging Roxy to stop, pulling on her collar, but she kept mauling Raffi like a crazy, possessed, maniacal demon.

Then as suddenly as it had started, it stopped. Roxy let Raffi go. He ran out the back door and under the house, where I believed he'd gone to die. I couldn't convince him to come out and fair enough. If you'd just been swung around like a rag doll in the mouth of your so-called best buddy, would you take that risk?

I went back into the hallway. It was a mess. The telephone was smashed and the spare double mattress we kept standing in our hallway had collapsed. I sat on the floor, wrapped my arms around my bent legs, put my head on my knees and wept. 'That fucking stupid spare mattress! Why can't we just have a nice, tartan foldout sofa bed like normal people? They're shithouse to sleep on, but they look nice.' I heard Roxy's paws pat, pat, pattering on the polished floorboards. I looked up to find her sitting close by, gazing at me. Her expression seemed to say, 'Golly, that was a bit full-on, wasn't it?' I knew I still loved Roxy but I was uncertain about what to do or how to handle her. I wondered if this was how Mrs Milat felt whenever her son Ivan dropped by for a cuppa.

Raffi lived. Like many dog fights it had looked and sounded much worse than it was; but still, it had been traumatic. Slowly, and with some expert help, we reintroduced the dogs and cautiously resumed life as normal.

Everyone I spoke to had a theory about how to separate fighting dogs. Of course there was the classic: 'Apparently, if you stick your finger up the aggressive dog's arse it will let go of its victim.' Well, of course it would! I think I'd be inclined to stop whatever I was doing if the same thing happened to me. I contemplated who might have discovered this theory, and in what circumstances. To be honest, I don't think it's natural. Who goes out for a walk in the park, sees a dog fight and, out of nowhere, decides to stick their finger up a dog's bottom? You see what I mean? It would certainly be a tricky one to explain to your family and friends.

A more viable, user-friendly strategy was to sprinkle pepper on the attacking dog's nose. And so I bought a small container of ground black pepper just in case.

A few weeks after the first attack, it happened again. This time the whole family witnessed it. We were watching TV together. The two dogs were lying on the floor snoozing when, once again with no warning, Roxy Girl started attacking Raffi. This time John tried to separate them. I screamed at Jordie, 'Quick, get the pepper off the bench!' He didn't know I'd bought the pre-ground stuff so he arrived with our large wooden pepper-grinder and, like an overzealous Italian waiter, started madly grinding peppercorns over Roxy's nose.

It worked. Once more Raffi lived, but this time it was clear: our two beloved dogs could never be in the same room again; one of them had to go. But which one? I hoped John would deal with it but the reality is that in many homes, when a shockingly brutal decision has to be made, and quick but painful action needs to be taken, it's the mums who rise to the occasion, just as my mum had all those years ago when she didn't have enough milk to make her tapioca pudding.

In the meantime we had to keep the dogs separated. Raffi would spend a couple of hours in the backyard while Roxy stayed in the house. Then one of us would have to hold onto Roxy and someone else would hold Raffi while they swapped locations.

John and I sought help from our local vet, who spent a lot of time with Roxy and decided that as long as she was in a one-dog home, she most likely would never attack again. And so I had to make the decision about which dog would stay and which would go. It was as if the dogs knew. They would both look at me with eyes that pleaded, 'Oh, please pick me, please ...' I felt like Meryl Streep in *Sophie's Choice*.

For three days and nights I tossed and turned and wept. On the fourth morning I announced to the family, 'We're keeping Raffi,' at which point I believe Raffi not only heard me but understood. On his face was an expression of shock; if he could speak he would've said, 'What? Who did she pick? Me? The little plain one? Oh my God, I don't believe it!' And he would've broken down and wept with relief. As it was, I was the one who once more broke into inconsolable sobs.

Here's a tip for nothing: if you ever want to experience firsthand the lowest form of scumbag, underbelly lowlife that Victoria has to offer, put an ad in the *Herald Sun* that starts with: 'Free to good home, staffy X.' I didn't know people trained them as fighting dogs.

But there were also some lovely people, like the extremely fit, articulate eighty-year-old chap whose friends thought he needed a dog. He lived in an immaculate upmarket house furnished with exquisite antiques. We took Roxy Girl to meet him and I believe she gave us her honest opinion on the matter when she proceeded to do a huge poo on the pure white carpet of his lounge room. This interview/selection process continued for three weeks. Finally, a family who lived on a large property in the country rang. They sounded great. But they had two kids aged about seven and five. I told them Roxy's history and, echoing the vet, they said they were sure Roxy would be absolutely fine with humans. The dad was going to be in Melbourne the next day so he called in to meet Roxy. They got on well. I agreed that he could have her and suggested that John and I drive Roxy Girl to their place the following weekend.

'But I can take her now,' he offered.

My stomach heaved. Tears welled up in my eyes. I bit my lip and said, 'Oh, yeah, okay then.' I walked Roxy out to the car and told her to climb into the back seat. I gave her new owner some of her food, her blanket and her bed. And as I watched the car drive away, tears streaming down my face, Roxy looked at me out the back window as if to say, 'See ya, Scotty, it's sure been swell, kid, it's been grand ...'

And as I feebly waved I couldn't help but picture Roxy dragging one of those kids around by their throat, and I wondered if perhaps I should have told them about the finger theory.

CHAPTER 17

Year 12, part one: the son

oubts about your child's education and future life prospects are not helped one little bit by the fact that every single year in early January the *Herald Sun* prints a listing of all Victorian secondary schools in order of their Year 12 academic achievement. This ranking is dictated by the results of the previous final year students. Thus, when Jordie was about to commence Year 12 and I read that his high school had come in at something like 389th out of 394, I panicked.

'John, John, are you awake? John. John. JOHN!'

'What, Scotty? What's wrong?'

'I can't sleep.'

'Why not?'

'Do you think we've fucked up our kids' lives?'

'What do you mean?'

'Do you think we should have sent them to private schools?'

'Scotty, you know what I think about private schools.'

'Tell me again …'

'I hate them. I hate their arrogance, I hate their sense of elitism and I hate the way they see themselves as above everyone else. I just hate them.'

'You can afford to, John. You went to Scotch College.'

It wasn't as if I wanted Jordie to become a doctor but I did want him to pass Year 12. I decided that instead of whinging and worrying I would become a proactive parent and take some positive action. After all, I'd been a Year 12 English teacher (albeit for one year some twenty years or so ago) and all my students had passed their English exam. (Admittedly, there were only four of them but a 100 per cent pass rate is a 100 per cent pass rate. Which makes me think that I must have been a damn-near brilliant teacher and, come to think of it, maybe I should have stuck with it. But now's not the time nor the place for career regrets.)

'Okay, Jordie, I reckon what you need is some exam practice, so here's the deal –'

'Mum, please –'

'Hear me out, Jords. What we're going to do is recreate exam conditions.'

'But Mum, we're at home.'

'Just pretend. Okay, you sit at your desk, I give you a sample question about one of your texts, set the timer for forty minutes, you write the answer and then we go through your paper together.'

'Mum, this isn't a good idea ...'

Ten minutes later Jordie was sitting at his desk looking decidedly unimpressed. We were both excellent at recreating an exam-type mood; the tension was palpable. I looked at the clock and announced in a very serious voice, 'Your time starts now.' Jordie gave me one of those you're-an-embarrassment-to-humankind looks.

I left the room and closed the door. I went into my office (since the renos I did indeed have a room of my own) and tried writing but I was too anxious. Jordie appeared at the study door.

'Mum, I can't do it.'

'Yes, you can.'

'No, I can't. I feel like I'm going to throw up.'

'That's good ...'

'That I'm going to throw up?'

'No, that you're facing your fears now instead of on the day of the exam.'

'No, Mum, this is making me feel worse. At least I would've gone into the exam thinking I could do it but now I know for sure that I can't.'

'Jordie, you need to go back into your room and just try to write something.'

'Like what?'

'I don't know, anything. Just start with a word and then add another one and see where it takes you.'

Jordie went back into his room. I was pretty darn impressed with myself. Who would've thought I had those spot-on words of wisdom just sitting there ready to roll when I needed them? God, I was good.

A minute later I walked past Jordie's door.

'I've written something, Mum.'

'Good on you.'

'Want to have a look?'

'Sure.'

He'd written one sentence: 'Year 12 is fucked.'

Adding to our anxiety was Jordie's announcement that he was NOT going to apply for any tertiary courses whatsoever. 'I want to be a contemporary muso. There's nowhere you can study that.'

'There are music courses.'

'I don't want to be taught how to do my music. Dylan never went to uni to learn how to write songs.'

'But what about that group Coldplay? I think they met at uni.'

'Whatever Mum. I hate Coldplay.'

And so I would lie in bed at night and worry about my firstborn leaving school and, and, and what? What would he do? Sure, he had his part-time dishwashing job but what about a career? What if he spent the year lying on the couch getting depressed; and then what if he couldn't snap out of the depression and would never, ever get a job; and what if he began to comfort eat, and he just kept getting fatter and fatter; and what if his skin actually fused to the couch; and what if the only way he could get out of the house was to have the roof taken off and a crane brought in; and what if, when he was finally lifted out of number 26, still fused to the couch, it was televised worldwide on Oprah Winfrey's show; and what if Oprah then organised for Bob Dylan to wander up to Jordie and play him a live version of 'Like a Rolling Stone' to try to get him off that couch; and what if everybody just wept at the tragedy of it all?

'Mum, you've got to have some faith in me. I know what I'm doing.'

'You're right, Jordie, it's your life.'

'Jordie, wake up. Jordie, WAKE UP.'

Jordie rubbed his eyes and blinked. 'Mum, what's up?'

'Today is the last day you can apply for that photography course at RMIT.'

'But Mum, I do not want to do a course.'

'I don't care. I want you to apply for something.'

'No, Mum …'

'Jordie, come next February, you may be very glad you've got somewhere to go.'

'Mum …'

'Alright then, *I'll* be glad you've got somewhere to go.'

Most kids turn eighteen when they're in Year 12, which allows them to legally drink in pubs until four in the morning, which means they don't wake up until at least three in the afternoon, usually with a disgusting hangover and suffering the ill-effects of a kebab from Gino's caravan at 3.30 am with double meat and garlic sauce. These are not the best conditions for coming to grips with the underlying themes in Patrick White's *The Tree of Man*. Which means they may not pass Year 12, which means that a mother lies in bed worrying that their child may lie on the couch and get depressed and get fat and have to get a crane ... it's a vicious circle.

Ironically, it was an incident that occurred in the early hours following Jordie's eighteenth birthday party that I believe played a big part in helping him focus on his exams and gain a healthy pass.

John and I were dreading hosting an eighteenth birthday party at our place. I would toss and turn in bed at night, and when I wasn't seeing Jordie being hoisted out through our roof I would see newspaper headlines: RESIDENTS FLEE HOMES AS GATECRASHERS AT EIGHTEENTH BIRTHDAY DESTROY ENTIRE CUL DE SAC.

So John and I did something quite unusual. We decided to make life easy on ourselves and hired a venue for Jordie's party. 'Oh John,' I sighed, as we lay in bed cocooned in the smugness that such a mature and sensible decision brings. 'Isn't it great knowing that someone else is going to do all the work? All we have to do is pay them.'

'Oh Scotty, it sure is,' said John. 'I love you, Scotty.'

'I love you, John.'

The inner-city streets and laneways of Melbourne are full of clubs, bars and restaurants featuring large, friendly signs that proudly declare: ROOM AVAILABLE FOR PRIVATE FUNCTIONS. ENQUIRE WITHIN. So that's just what we did.

'Hi there. Yes, look, we want to hire a venue for a party, for about one hundred or so people,' John began.

And the venue owner's eyes would light up, ringing with dollar signs like fruit on a pokies machine. 'Come with me,' he'd say, 'we've just had upstairs renovated and it is gorgeous. Who's the lucky one having the party, then?'

'It's our son Jordie. It's his eighteenth.'

The venue owner would stop dead in his tracks. 'Eighteenth? It's an eighteenth birthday party? Oh, we don't do eighteenths. We did once, but never again. You've never seen so much vomit.'

'Oh, I think we might have,' I'd venture in a jocular way, but I'd stop myself before adding, 'but that was at my son's fifteenth.'

Everywhere we went the response was much the same. As soon as we said the word 'eighteenth' people would reel back in horror, pull down their shades, shut the door and put a closed sign in their window.

But sometimes life deals you a lucky card and eventually we found a venue that was more than happy to host an eighteenth birthday party; in fact, they seemed downright enthusiastic about having the place full of young people. In retrospect, maybe this had something to do with the fact that less than two weeks after Jordie's party, the venue was raided and the owner and his staff arrested for dealing cocaine and selling alcohol to minors. As John said, 'Phew, lucky we got in before they closed the place down, hey?'

The morning after the party, Jordie awoke only to have his friend Christo, who was sleeping on the floor, say, 'Fuckin' hell, Jordie, what the fuck?'

Jordie looked down at his right leg. 'Shit, fuckin' hell.'

Oh yes, Year 12 had certainly done a lot to improve the articulation skills of these young lads.

(I must acknowledge that the sarcasm in this last comment may seem a little harsh, especially since it was me who made up those last two quotes. I had to; obviously I wasn't in the bedroom when the interaction took place. However, I've since checked with both my sources and Christo and Jordie agreed that I 'totally nailed' their conversation, which makes my sarcasm perfectly justified after all.)

There was a massive blister on Jordie's shinbone, quite literally the size of a softball. John immediately hauled him into the Camry and they headed off to a deeply depressed, extremely annoyed, bulk-billing, fill-in doctor who was reluctantly working the Sunday shift. In fact, so profound was this doctor's disappointment with the current state of his career that John believed, without doubt, it was the reason Jordie was left with a large, ugly, permanent scar on his shin.

Apparently, the doctor had simply looked at Jordie's leg and flatly declared that it was 'probably a white-tip spider bite', at which point, without fanfare or warning, he'd produced a needle and brutally popped the massive blister, which by now was the size of a basketball. He then cleaned the wound with the same intensity you'd use to sand back floorboards.

Jordie returned home in quite a state of excitement, declaring, 'So that's why I was so sick last night, a white-tip spider bite!'

I vividly recalled seeing Jordie at his party towards the end of the night. He was sitting in one of the booths surrounded by a bevy of young, beautiful girls. These gorgeous young creatures were all wearing strapless or halter-neck tops, tight skirts, and those who had naturally curly hair wore it straight, and those who had naturally straight hair wore it curly. Their skin glistened with golden spray-on tans, they wore high-heeled shoes that showed off their painted toenails, and they were massaging Jordie's shoulders, his back, his neck, fussing and purring words of love and encouragement. But there was one girl who was obviously queen bee because she had *the gig*, you know, *the top gig*, *the gig* they all craved; it was she who got to kneel at Jordie's feet, holding aloft a big, ornate, silver ice-bucket for him to vomit into.

And so here we were the following day with Jordie claiming that passing out unconscious in a gutter was, in fact, the fault of a white-tip spider.

Whatever the real story, we'll never know. But one thing was blatantly obvious: over the next couple of weeks the red, raw welt on Jordie's leg turned a sort of greenish-brown and was producing enough pus daily to fill a teacup. Eventually antibiotics were prescribed by a different doctor, this time a happy doctor who appeared to care. One round of antibiotics did nothing. So Jordie took another round. They were long rounds, virtually taking him right up to the start of his VCE exams. What a marvellous coincidence. In fact, if I ever met this white-tip spider, I would thank it.

Because we all know that you can't drink alcohol while taking antibiotics. Well, I took this a step further and informed Jordie: 'No doctor's ever going to tell you this, but if you do drink alcohol while taking antibiotics you could die. This happened to a friend of a friend of mine so please, do not drink any alcohol whatsoever while on these tablets or else you could DIE.'

Jordie stopped drinking completely, passed his VCE exams and was accepted into the photography course. It was listed in the paper. All his friends were mystified, 'Gee, Jord, we never knew you wanted to do photography …' True to his word, he did not accept the offer and just as I imagined, he took up residency on the couch.

CHAPTER 18

Year 12, part two: the daughter

t was a Sunday afternoon in early November. I was sitting in the kitchen when I heard Bonnie running up and down the hallway cussing, as Dr Phil might say. She was to sit her Year 12 visual communication exam the next day.

To be honest, I didn't know exactly what visual communication was. I did know that at one stage it involved designing and making a shoebox, and that the day before this shoebox was due to be handed in for assessment, the tension had brought my eyeballs to the verge of popping out of their sockets, pushing me very close to grabbing Bonnie by her shoulders and slapping her face for her own good. Instead I called a cab, and in an extremely pinched, almost strangulated voice that was heading towards hysteria, I told the driver, 'This is an emergency.' It was approximately 4.40 pm and we had to be at a printer's in Collingwood before they closed at 5 pm. In perfect driving conditions, this trip takes between fifteen or twenty minutes. But it was peak hour.

Our mission was to pick up a large print-out of Bonnie's original graphic design which she would then use to cover her unique shoebox, which she still had to make that evening. My worst fears were now being realised as we were indeed caught in peak-hour traffic. Bonnie was looking out the cab window quietly crying, knowing that if she didn't hand in the shoebox she wouldn't be assessed and therefore she would fail and therefore the rest of her life would be ruined. In my own anxiety attack, I was torn between feeling sorry for Bonnie and desperately wanting to ask her through gritted teeth, 'Why in God's name don't you do these things a little ahead of time?' Oh no, now we had become stuck in a gridlock situation.

Oh Jesus Christ, move. Someone, anyone, just please move. I considered suggesting to Bonnie that we abandon the cab and run the remaining three kilometres. Even though we couldn't possibly have made it in time, at least we would have been moving as opposed to sitting powerless inside a cab watching the metre tick over while we went absolutely nowhere. I wanted to scream.

The taxi-driver, a cool, black African dude, was playing reggae music. I considered asking him to turn it off as its laid-back vibe was making it hard for me to concentrate on my stress. He asked me what was wrong. Once he realised the dramatic life-and-death nature of the situation, and the fact that I didn't have a mobile phone (as usual, Bonnie's had run out of credit) he used his phone to ring the printers and then handed it to me. I begged them to stay open until we got there. The woman on the other end seemed unimpressed until I explained, 'It's for my daughter's Year 12 assignment, it's due –'

She cut me off. 'Say no more. My son did VCE last year. We'll stay open until you get here.'

The woman at the printer's handed over the enormous roll of paper, which was now covered in Bonnie's original artwork. She complimented Bonnie, saying the design was, 'Marvellous. What's it for?'

'I'm covering a shoebox,' Bonnie replied without much confidence.

'Oh, good luck,' said the woman, not sounding overly confident herself.

We got back in the cab. Our cool dude turned up the reggae and we had ourselves a mini celebration. The round trip, including a tip, cost $75; the roll of paper, $120. When we were back inside the house, Bonnie burst into tears again. 'I'm sorry, Mum, for all the money I'm costing you.' I didn't bother telling her that at that stage I would have gladly given away our house if it meant she would successfully complete the shoebox by the next day.

Bonnie then retreated to her room where she began the actual construction of the box. Hours went by. John and I waited nervously in the lounge area. It was after midnight when she finally emerged from her room, once more in tears. 'But Bonnie, it's brilliant!' John declared with absolute conviction. He studied it closely. 'Wow, Bonnie, it's absolutely superb!' He turned it over to view the other side. 'It's fantastic. I love the handle. So easy to carry, and the central opening system is so clever. And the artwork, Bonnie, it's just so cool.'

'Yeah, Bonnie, it's really good,' I lamely offered. I'm not very good at praising my children, which in this instance was a shame because without doubt it was a great box.

'But look how big it is,' Bonnie sobbed. 'Who would ever have feet that big?'

Bonnie did have a point. The box *was* big. 'You could call it The Shaquille O'Neal Shoebox' John jovially suggested. Bonnie ran from the room crying.

The next morning, her eyes puffy and red, she headed off with the shoebox, knowing that her life was finished. A few days later she arrived home beaming. She'd got an A+ for the box. Not only that, but the teacher had used it as an example of truly innovative design work. I went to a nearby bar and had a few drinks by myself to celebrate. After all, a victory for your child is a victory for you.

But now here we were, the day before her final visual communication exam. And once more Bonnie was in tears. I could hear her throwing things around in her room, not aggressively, but as though she was searching for something. God help her if that was the case. Bonnie's room was so messy I couldn't remember if she had polished boards or carpet.

I was sitting at the kitchen table in a state of mild paralysis. My stomach was knotted, my shoulders stiff, and I wished like hell that I still smoked. As the mother of a young girl in a state of extreme agitation, I wanted with all my heart to help alleviate her pain but what could I do?

'Dear God, I know it's been a long time but I need your help, not for me, for my daughter. Could you please, please, please help her pass her VCE exams?'

I knew that the correct protocol was to offer God some sort of sacrifice to secure the deal. When I was at my all-girl Catholic school, I once gave up eating choc-mint sundae biscuits for Lent, although this was more to do with wanting to clear up my pimples than serving God. If I seriously wanted God to help Bonnie out, I needed to give up something I seriously loved.

'Dear God, if Bonnie passes her exams I'll give up drinking wine.'

A mother's love can be pretty impressive. But soon I had to renege on this offer when I found myself hoping that Bonnie wouldn't pass so that I could keep drinking. Bonnie was on her own.

Bonnie's dream, her goal, her sole focus for years, had been to do a degree in visual arts at one of Melbourne's prestigious art schools. There was nothing else she wanted; it was her Holy Grail. Her practical work was certainly good enough. My personal favourites were her portraits of John – large drawings entitled 'Man with Eyebrows' and 'Man without Eyebrows', a snapshot of John before and after alopecia.

Exams, for Bonnie, were torture. Given the choice between doing a visual communication exam and having chopsticks inserted in both ears and slowly twisted (which is what the nuns at my school told us would happen when, not if, the communists invaded) Bonnie would have gone the chopsticks option for sure. In fact, in a moment of unselfish, motherly love, I would've offered to take the chopsticks for her 'if only you will please let my daughter go to art school'. Oh dear, at this point even I was confused as it now appeared I was praying to the Chinese communists to help my daughter.

I wished I could do what my own mother did for me all those years ago back in '72 as I lay sobbing on my pink chenille bedspread, having just returned from my Year 12 English exam. I was inconsolable. 'Mum, I completely stuffed up.' (Obviously Marg wasn't as tolerant of her children using obscene language.) 'I was too tired. I didn't sleep at all last night. I just lay there, Mum. And now I'm not going to sleep for the rest of my exams and I'm so tired, and I've worked so hard, and all I want to do is go to uni, and now I won't be able to, and what will I do then?'

'You could always do nursing.' This was Mum's solution to just about everything. In fact, I think John was in his forties when she suggested the same thing to him.

'I don't want to do nursing, Mum. I wanted to be a social worker but now ...' And I continued to weep into my pillow, my glow-in-the-dark crucifix staring at me from its central position on the dressing table.

I'm not simply trying to justify my emotional breakdown when I say that the Catholic church had recently undergone some major changes and the fall-out was still wreaking havoc. Sister Mary Margaret Maria Goretti had become Sister Sue. The veils changed to smaller models so that now you could see some of the nuns' hair. This small concession meant that one evening, when for some reason I was forced to knock on the convent door, I was horrified to see our head nun answer wearing a hair-curler in her fringe.

The entire matric year, as it was known back then, had been somewhat of a disaster. Our English expression teacher, who I loved and who in turn championed my work, giving me A or A+ for every essay, suicided in the April of that year. She was replaced by, well it doesn't matter who, what mattered was that this new teacher hated my work and proceeded to give me E for my essays.

Our biology teacher was my first encounter with a total charlatan. He knew nothing about biology, nothing at all, not so much as the slightest idea of how to turn on a Bunsen burner. He'd been a truck-driver until he got the gig teaching at our school. Maybe it was his exotic American accent that won over the nuns and their newly curled fringes. It certainly wasn't his looks. He was a scrawny runt who from the front looked like a shifty,

Dickensian weasel and from the back resembled a wire coat-hanger with a crumpled suit hanging on it. It was rumoured that he smoked dope and had sex with students in the dark room. One day, out of the blue, he was sacked; thank God. But he was never replaced. This meant I had to teach myself all about parthenogenesis and was amazed to learn that sometimes lady turkeys don't need a man turkey to fertilise their eggs. They can do it all on their own. What a concept: being able to reproduce without having to have sex with a man! I recalled the image of my biology teacher and thought what a welcome relief that would be.

But my favourite bit of weirdness for the year was when we were informed that our history teacher, let's call her Miss Lewis, had to suddenly resign. At around the same time, one of the Year 12 girls, let's call her Catherine, also quit school and was said to have run away from home.

Now it may seem obvious where this story is heading but I hope there's still a little sting in the tail that will surprise. It certainly surprised us Year 12 girls.

A couple of weeks after running away, Catherine contacted a few of her friends from school and asked if we wanted to meet with her. A date, place and time were arranged. We girls rocked up at the agreed venue and sure enough, there was Catherine. Everyone hugged and kissed and then Catherine announced that she would like us to meet her new boyfriend, at which point 'he' emerged from behind a bush. It was Miss Lewis. No surprises there perhaps, but Miss Lewis was wearing men's clothes and had swept up her longish hair under a pork-pie hat. But the bit that really got me was that Miss Lewis was wearing a fake moustache and was introduced to us as Brian. Evidently, neither Catherine nor Miss Lewis thought that anyone would guess that 'Brian' was really the woman who, only two weeks earlier, had been standing in front of our history class wearing a skirt and high heels, explaining the events of the Eureka stockade.

On the last day of the school year before breaking for exams, the Year 12s celebrated by riding two-wheeler bikes covered in crepe paper to school – as they say, when Catholic girls go off, we really go off. On the way we called in at my friend Anne's house to pick her up. Anne explained that she wasn't allowed to come to school that day. She'd been banned by the nuns because the school's master key had been stolen the night before and she was the accused. Anne was one of the most popular girls at school. She assured us that she hadn't stolen the key and her word was good enough for me. It was good enough for all of us, so an outraged group of seventeen-year-old Catholic girls pedalled off on our crepe paper–covered bikes determined that justice would be done.

At school, during our barbecue breakfast on the basketball court, I was elected spokesperson for the 'Save Anne' committee. Our head nun was in a classroom on her own doing some work at her table. I gently knocked on the door. 'Excuse me, Sister Judy, I'm sorry to interrupt, but may I please speak with you?'

Sister Judy smiled kindly and beckoned me in. Quite frankly, I think she was probably grateful for the acknowledgement; usually we paid her no attention whatsoever. I explained, with utter conviction, that Anne had not stolen the key and that it was cruel and unfair not to allow her to celebrate the last day of school with the rest of us.

Sister Judy looked at me, a crazy smile on her face. Slowly she began to stand, her hands clutching the table in front of her, all the while staring at me. She stood upright for a few seconds and then I noticed her body beginning to twitch. It then developed into a full-on spasmodic shaking, her glasses went skew-whiff and froth started bubbling out of her huge, buck-toothed mouth. I stood there watching in horror as she then fell to the floor and lay there sobbing and writhing and convulsing in a state such as I'd never witnessed.

Soon after, we watched our head nun carried out the school gate on a stretcher. The term 'nervous breakdown' was being whispered in hushed tones. Anne was allowed to come back to school. We never saw Sister Judy again.

That's part of the reason I was lying on my chenille bedspread weeping, knowing that the odds were against any of us passing those exams; at the time this meant my entire life would be ruined. I heard Mum leave the house. Thirty minutes later she returned. She came into my bedroom and without a word handed me a brown paper bag. I opened it. Inside was a packet of Relaxa-tabs. Mum had bought them over the counter, no script required; ah, those were the days. They worked immediately. I mean *immediately*. As soon as I looked at the packet and read its promise of eight hours' sleep, I instantly relaxed. God, they were good. In fact, I still recall those fourteen days in the early summer of '72 as the best period of sleep I've ever had in my entire insomnia–ridden life.

But here we were in November 2004, the day before Bonnie's visual communication exam. I repeat and underline that it was November. 'Oh shit, shit, shit … fucking hell … where are they?' Bonnie's voice was quavering, her sense of panic rising. I knocked on her bedroom door and went in. I considered kicking the clothes and objects that were strewn across the floor out of the way as I walked towards her bed but decided to use Bonnie's technique and walked straight over the top of them.

'Bonnie, what is wrong?' (I know, what an amazing question. I swear I didn't get it out of a 'how to parent' manual but thought it up myself.)

Bonnie whimpered, 'It's my visual communication exam tomorrow and I've lost all my notes. All of them. I can't find them anywhere.'

'Look, Bonn, just calm down, they must be here somewhere. Just think. When did you last see them?'

'February,' she replied without hesitation. It was at this point I knew there was nothing any of us could do to help.

CHAPTER 19

Working with your offspring

hy would any mother choose to do a show in the Melbourne International Comedy Festival with her nineteen-year-old son? Well, 'desperation' is the first word that springs to mind. I was at a bit of a loose end. I felt like my career was heading nowhere and I wanted to do something significant, something risky, something I'd never done before. As for Jordie, he'd spent the previous year after finishing high school, as predicted, lying on the couch, wondering how he could achieve his dreams.

'Ma, how do reckon you get started in the music industry?'

I replied with a mother's innate wisdom, 'I wouldn't have a clue.' I paused before continuing, 'But there is one thing I do know and it is this. You have to get up off the couch and walk out the front door.'

A pause to consider the true meaning of such a deep and enlightening statement. 'And?'

'And what?'

'Well, what do I do once I'm out the front door?'

'I don't know. That's not the point. What I do know is that nothing is going to happen while you hang around here. You've got to go forth and see where life takes you.'

Minutes later Jordie rose from the couch – fantastic; for once it was vacant and I could lie down – and he walked out the front door. Fifteen minutes later he was back. Life had taken him to the local bakery, where he'd bought a meat pie.

Thus, I decided to do a show with Jordie to get him off the couch. Oh, and I was fully aware that he was a major musical talent. And I was fully aware that a mother–son comedy show would make a brilliant marketing strategy. And I was fully aware that I often struggled to attract audiences to my shows and that having a young, talented, good-looking male muso may help.

But the real reason I decided to perform a show with Jordie was because my comedy buddy, Lynda Gibson, was dying. Ovarian cancer had decided her fate, and before departing this earth she gave me three farewell gifts that without doubt inspired me to exploit my firstborn. And inadvertently, he helped me through my grief.

The first gift Lynda gave me was love. It sounds corny and clichéd but that is what I received from her in her last few months — love and only love. It was the only thing that was important to her. Crusty, cranky, red wine–loving Lynda Gibson, famous for her negativity and loved for it because there was no one funnier when she was going mad about comedy, politics and life in general, had become, in those last few months, the Mahatma Gandhi of West Preston. (This wasn't so much due to her spiritual development but to her legs, which bore an uncanny resemblance to the Mahatma's.) Daily we would gather around Lynda as she held court on her back porch. We had to sit on her porch because even though Lynda could no longer eat, drink or walk very easily, she still had the guts, strength and determination to get outside and have a cigarette.

The second gift Lynda gave me was the same message I received the night my dad died: 'Life is too short. There is no time to muck around. If you want to do something, do it now.' Sure, this is a message you often hear but when it comes from a person who, for whatever reason, is leaving this earth and, for whatever reason, you get to stay, you feel more compelled to heed the advice. I'd been contemplating doing a show with Jordie for ages but had done nothing about it. Now was the time.

This lesson led to Lynda's third and most unusual gift. Being aware that life is short, I got up the courage to ask Kevin Whyte to manage me. As far as comedy management goes, you can't get better than Kev. It took courage to ask him because I'd already approached him once and he'd said no. Kev was a friend of Lynda's and had been helping out a great deal in those last few months so I'd seen quite a bit of him. In some ways this made asking him easier but I also knew that it would make rejection just that little bit more awkward.

'Guess what, Lynda?'

'What?'

'I asked Kevin Whyte if he would manage me.'

'And?'

'He said yes.'

In her weakened voice, Lynda could barely manage more than a whisper, 'Scotty, that is great news, really great news.'

I was lying on the bed beside Lynda at her home in Preston. We were holding hands and staring up at the ceiling. A minute of contemplative silence followed.

'You know why he said yes, don't you, Scotty?'

'Why?'

'Because I'm dying.'

'You don't think it might be because of my talent?'

'Nuh. He feels sorry for you because your best friend is dying.'

We grinned. Maybe there was some truth to the theory.

'Think of it as my parting gift to you.'

'It's a great gift, Lynda, thank you.'

'My pleasure, Scotty.'

★

So there I was in my brand-new comedy manager's upstairs office in downtown Brunswick Street, Fitzroy. It was a hot, summery day in late 2003. I was waiting to have a meeting with Kev. He was on the phone and called out, 'Important call, Scotty, won't be long.'

'Not a problem, Kev.'

To be honest, I didn't have anywhere I had to absolutely be until, mmm ... let's see, the following year, I guess. I studied the photos of the comics Kev represented sitting happily inside nice gold frames on the wall. Yes, they were very successful people, yep, they certainly were, no doubt about that. I wondered who Kev was talking to; probably someone in the States, or maybe he was stitching up a TV deal, or getting someone out of a contract, or booking someone into rehab; all those things that managers do. Yeah, anyway. Oh God, I was nervous.

I was waiting to meet with Kev and his cousin Kathleen because as part of managing me they'd offered to produce my Melbourne Comedy Festival show. This was an unbelievably joyous prospect. For years I'd had to produce all my own shows and, apart from shelling out lots of money, it meant having to constantly call on favours from friends and family, asking them to do stuff for you for nothing. Well, not exactly for nothing. One year I offered John sexual favours if he managed to bring over a hundred people to my show on opening night. My fellow local comics were shaking their heads in amazement and disbelief, muttering, 'Did you hear? Scotty sold out opening night. How does she do it? She hasn't even got a publicist!'

But here I was, about to meet with Kev and Kath. I entered Kev's office. He was standing by his open window, sucking really hard on his cigarette and then swinging around and hanging out the window to exhale – at which point the hot breeze would blow the smoke back inside again. Kev leaned back against the windowsill, pushed his groovy dark-framed glasses up his nose and went into serious manager mode, talking about budgets and percentages and breakdowns of box-office takings. I didn't understand a word of it, but I was pretty certain that it didn't involve me having to offer sexual favours in return. Kath was sitting at the table, spiral notebook and pen in hand. She looked serious. The time was fast approaching when Kev would stop talking and I would have to pitch my idea for a show. And Kev and Kath would have to like it. Oh dear.

I had two ideas. The first was doing the show with Jordie, the second was to finally realise an ambition and perform a solo stand-up show which I'd never done in the festival; I'd always gone for something more theatrical. I decided to pitch the solo idea first. I took a deep breath, waited for Kev to stop hanging out the window, and away I went.

'You know, I'm, well, getting close to forty-nine now, and what I've always wanted to do is what, you know, lots of comedians do; I just want to do a stand-up show, just me and a mike. No theme, no props, no gimmicks. Just gags ...' I paused. Kev and Kath were overwhelmingly silent. I knew I was losing them. By now Kev was hanging out the window again.

'I have had another idea. I've thought for some time about doing a show with my nineteen-year-old son.' Kev's head immediately appeared back inside the room. I knew I was onto something; the ball was in my hands and I was going to run with it. 'Yeah, I mean, he finished Year 12 a year ago and look, he's a really talented muso ...' I don't quite understand how ears prick up but I believe Kev's and Kath's ears did exactly that when they heard the mention of a nineteen-year-old guy who was also a musician.

'What sort of music?'

'His own original songs – ballads, country, blues, rock, pop; all sorts.'

'Does he play an instrument?'

'Yeah. He's an excellent guitarist.'

'Electric?'

'Electric and acoustic.'

Kev nodded in an I'm-thinking-this-is-a-good-idea sort of way, and this time he didn't even bother to exhale out the window but blew the smoke out the corner of his mouth.

'Yeah, so I thought I could write a show about the relationship between a mother and her young son; I'd do the comedy stuff and Jord would write the music and do the songs.'

Kath stopped me right there. 'Sounds fabulous, what do you think, Kev?'

'Fucking great. So all you've got to do now is go home and write the show. We'll do the rest.'

I went home. Jordie was lying on the couch watching *Passions*, a particularly bad/good (depending on what you're looking for) American soap that screened at three o'clock every weekday. I sat down on the foldout leopard-skin camping chair, which we'd produced from the shed some years earlier when we'd had a lot of people over and hadn't got around to putting back. I told Jordie the good news. He was dubious. 'I don't know, Ma; I'm a musician, not a comedian.'

A week or so later at Lynda's wake, a journalist in her early forties who had long sexy legs, wore a short, funky mini and had had a few drinks cornered Jordie and complimented him on his singing during the funeral service. She then purred huskily, 'And Jordie, I hear you're doing the Comedy Festival; you are *soooo* going to get laid.' At this moment Jordie fully committed to the project.

Okay, rightio, now all we had to do was write the show – together. Gulp. Where to start? Okay, I had to get a grip, I was the grown-up, I was the experienced comedian. I had to take the lead. Yep. Alright. It was up to me. I had to initiate ... something. Okay, let's see, first things first, um ... I know, a diary meeting, yes, that's it, we'll have a diary meeting and work out a writing and rehearsal schedule.

'Okay Jordie, the diary meeting is going to be at 10.30 tomorrow morning.'

'10.30? Shit, that's early.'

'Jordie, we've got a lot to do. Are you going to be there at 10.30 or not?'

'Yeah, yeah, chill out, Ma, don't get so stressed, I'll be there. But you might have to wake me up.'

'Jordie, I'm not going to wake you up to come to rehearsals. We're not mother and son now, we're professional work colleagues.'

'Yeah, I know, I'm just saying I mightn't wake up.'

'And I'm saying you just have to. And it's not as if you've got far to go. All you have to do is roll out of bed and keep rolling and bingo you'll be at work. Okay, so we're agreed, 10.30 tomorrow morning in my office?'

'Yep, I'll be there, Ma.'

At 11.30 the following morning I was sitting in my office listening to Jordie's alarm beeping like a massive truck reversing down an eighty-six kilometre driveway. While the sound of it inspired an energetic desire on my part to march into Jordie's room and hurl the clock radio at the wall, it did nothing more than rouse Jordie to extend his arm and turn on the snooze button. I was determined not to go in and scream, 'For God's sake,

your mother's career is at stake. GET OUT OF BED!'
And so I waited.

At 11.45 I heard a thud as Jordie hit the floor; evidently
he did just roll across the hallway and into my office
because there he was, sleep sticking his eyes together, his
hair sweaty, matted and flattened, wearing nothing but a
T-shirt and his old boxers.

'Shit, Ma, sorry. I'm just, I don't know, I think there
might be something wrong with me. Seriously, Ma, I
think I must have a sleeping disorder or something, I
just feel really weird.'

'Maybe it's because you stayed up until 4.30 this
morning?'

'Don't get sarcastic, Ma. I'm serious; I think there
could be something really wrong with me. Anyway, is it
okay if I have a shower? I've got to wake up, and I
wouldn't mind having something to eat.'

The next day we started developing the basic show
outline that I'd been working on over the previous
month. We sat opposite each other at a table in my office.
Boy oh boy, this was awkward, weird, in fact it was a
babushka doll situation. How often do you get to write a
show with a person who once lived inside you? Not often
at all. And he was so tall! So tall and grown-up. He was
an adult, this person sitting opposite me, a grown-up man
with the beginnings of a beard. A beard? When did he
start having all that facial hair? Who the hell was this
guy? I didn't know him at all. Did he ever do drugs? Was

he in love with a girl? Was he gay? There was no indication of this but you never know. Was he happy? Or sad? Or depressed? Or nervous about having to sit opposite me and write a comedy show? If he was with his mates instead of with me what would he be talking about? Girls maybe, drugs, parties, alcohol, hopes, dreams, sex ... But this wasn't Jordie and his mates, this was Jordie and his mother, and we had to create a show together and this involved talking to each other and maybe even arguing, which was something I'd never really done with my kids. This was awkward enough for me, but what must it have been like for Jordie? I could only imagine. Maybe he was wishing he'd done that photography course after all.

Co-writing a script can often be tricky. Having to tell someone that you think their idea isn't up to scratch can be hard, but when it's your son, the child whose paintings you pinned up on the fridge, the child whose clay sculpture of an elephant's foot you've still got on the shelf in the lounge room, the child you gushed over for simply having a go at cross-country running even though he vomited before the finish line; when you have to tell this same person that you think his fart joke is quite literally a stinker, it can be tricky, that's all I'm saying.

I confess I wasn't very direct when giving Jordie critical feedback. I preferred a more subtle approach.

'What, Ma?'

'What do you mean what?'

'Ma, you sighed.'

'So?'

'Well, what?'

'Nothing.'

'Ma, why don't you just say it?'

'Say what?'

'Why don't you just say, "Fart jokes are immature, Jordie?"'

'Alright, I'll say it. Fart jokes are immature, Jordie.'

But much to my shock and horror, the critical feedback response was a two-way street. Can you believe it? My nineteen-year-old son criticising me! Hello, I'd been doing comedy for twenty years and there I was suggesting a joke and ...

'I don't get it.'

'You don't get what?'

'I don't get your joke.'

'Well, that doesn't matter.'

'Yes, it does.'

'Alright then,' and I would explain the joke.

'I still don't get it.'

I would start explaining it again.

'No, Ma, I get the joke but I guess my point is I don't think it's funny.'

Family rifts have never healed over a lot less.

With the help of a director, Russell Fletcher, we finally got the show together and had a trial run a couple of weeks before our opening night. It stank. Yep, it really did. This had been my ultimate dread. To have your own turkey of a show is one thing but to drag your offspring with you down the stinking cesspit of comedy failure is hideous. As a mother your natural inclination is to protect your child, not to do an Abraham and carry your firstborn up to the top of a mountain, tie him to a pile of highly flammable kindling and burn him to death as a sacrifice to God. Of course, in Abraham's case God intervened and he didn't have to slaughter his son after all. But hey, if you were Abraham's child, would you ever walk up a mountain with your dad again? Not likely.

Making our situation even worse was Jordie's conviction that the show had gone great. He was beaming, 'It was fantastic, don't you reckon, Ma?'

I looked at his cherubic face and tried to be as gentle and sensitive as possible. 'Jords,' I said, 'it stank.'

His face fell. 'What are we going to do?'

'We're going to rewrite the show.'

'No way, Ma, I can't do that. How will I ever learn the new lines?'

I explained that doing a show six nights a week for a month that was a stinker and that you were responsible for – as in you'd WRITTEN it and you PERFORMED it – was a particularly hideous experience that could destroy your self-belief for, well, forever, and so had to be avoided at all costs.

Jordie, Russell and I reworked the show. At the same time we were on the publicity trail doing many radio interviews together. People loved the idea of Jordie being in the show and he quickly learnt the art of sounding as though he knew what he was doing – talking it up when in fact neither of us had a clue whether it was going to work at all. Jordie was also introduced to the world of breakfast radio: high-octane funny presenters who would ask if I still breastfed Jordie, and why we didn't call the show 'Step-ho and Son'? Welcome to the world of comedy, son.

Opening night arrived and Jordie and I got to the 'theatre' early. It was actually a hotel and we were to perform in a function room that seated about 180 people. Three shows were booked in that room each night. The show before ours was Sancia Robinson's poignant account of her battles with eating disorders. That first night Jordie and I were let in a back entrance; we sneaked up the grungy back stairs and changed into our costumes. Jordie wore a daggy blue suit while I donned a long, blue, kitsch, sequined, stretch-fabric evening frock.

We were waiting out the back, nervously listening to Sancia throwing up on stage when Jordie whispered, 'Ma, I want to go to the toilet.' We couldn't find one backstage. Our search became more and more frantic as Jordie became more and more desperate. He ran downstairs only to return a minute later with the tragic news that the door was deadlocked. We couldn't get out. The only exit available was walking across the stage, past Sancia, and out through her audience to the door. This would have been unforgivable. Jordie looked stricken. He was now jigging from foot to foot like a distressed tribal rain-dancer. This was the sort of thing a mother should have a solution for; admittedly, not usually when your child is nineteen years old.

And then Jordie saw it: a Corningware casserole dish. For all we knew, it may have been one of Sancia's props but this was an emergency. Jordie hid in the stairwell, returning a few minutes later with another interesting query: 'What will I do with it now?'

That's when I declared, 'Jordie, I don't know.' It was a defining moment. As a caring mother, I should have at least helped my son figure out what to do with his baking dish of urine but at that point in time I wasn't his mother. I was a comedian preparing to go on stage and I had other things on my mind. I have absolutely no idea how he solved his problem. But if you're ever in an inner-city Melbourne hotel and you spot a Corningware casserole dish suspiciously lurking behind a curtain or under a staircase, best leave it be.

For the following four weeks, at seven o'clock every evening except Mondays, I would announce, 'Jordie, we have to go.' And every evening Jordie would be running late, so I would then announce, 'Okay Jordie, I'm going.' I would then proceed to walk to the tram stop. I'd be carrying my own gear plus one of Jordie's guitars, usually the electric one because it was heavier than the acoustic and Jordie had a sore back. I would almost be at the tram stop when Jordie would come rushing past me with his youthful vigour. 'Come on, Ma, hurry up, the tram's coming!' Sitting on the tram, we'd go through the show together; at the venue we'd get ready and do a high-five before we went on stage.

'Scotty and Son' went well. It was a real turning point for both of us. It was the year my son discovered the Comedy Festival bar, embracing it as only a nineteen-year-old can. It was the year I stopped going to the Comedy Festival bar as only a responsible, ageing mother of an enthusiastic nineteen-year-old can. How could I possibly hang out and drink with the same people as my son? It felt wrong. Put simply, there wasn't enough room for both of us so I would head home on the tram at around 9.30, leaving my son to discover the underbelly of the Melbourne comedy scene.

I would sit on the tram and gaze out the window and wonder why life turns out the way it does. I'd contemplate how I'd started comedy as a 34-year-old with a 'husband' and two young children so I'd never got into the late-night drinking party scene; consequently, I'd never really felt I belonged. And now here was my son embracing it to such an extent that I was almost resentful of him. For God's sake, what the hell was I doing going home on the tram at 9.30 to have a cup of tea and go to bed when my son was out partying at the festival club with all the comedians? How weird. How bizarre. How Hollywood. I was like Dina Lohan, Lindsay's mum, without the tan, the botox, the good teeth or the stick-thin figure. I was resenting my own child's youth. I was resenting his freedom. I was resenting the passing of time, which left me facing the harsh reality: I was a tubby woman, approaching fifty, who'd had to use her own child to lure an audience to her Comedy Festival show.

Of course, there was another reason I was heading home early. Lynda. She wasn't there. She'd been at every single Comedy Festival since it started in 1987. Only the year before, Lynda had been performing with me and Judith Lucy in a show called 'Comedy Is Still Not Pretty'. Lynda was on a cocktail of cancer drugs and often in extreme pain, which she never referred to. She didn't have to. Breaking out into a sweat, her face would suddenly go taut and she'd grab onto a chair and steel herself against the unbearable surges of pain, her wispy tufts of chemo hair sticking to her scalp. And yet, she loved being in that show. So did Judith and I. Performing together in what turned out to be Lynda's last Comedy Festival rates as one of the greatest privileges life has afforded me.

But now Lynda was gone and for that matter so was Judith – she'd moved to Sydney to work on a commercial breakfast radio show. (Or, as I used to explain in 'Scotty and Son', 'In other words, Lynda's gone to heaven and Judith's gone to hell.')

Jordie understood my loss. In fact, he did more than understand. He felt my loss. Maybe it was because we were family. Whatever the reason, it was weird and unexpected how my nineteen-year-old son unwittingly became a real rock for me during this time. I gained enormous strength and comfort from doing the show with him.

And there was the added bonus that it was successful. We sold out every night. The media were really interested and we were nominated for the Barry Award (best show in the festival).

Nevertheless, we ended our show with a song whose final words were: 'We will never, ever, ever do a show together again.' And we haven't. And we won't.

Purely out of curiosity, I recently asked my son, 'When was the last time you cried?'

'On the last night of the Comedy Festival, the year I did the show with you,' he replied. I was touched. He continued, 'Yeah, it was eight o'clock in the morning and I was the last one left at the festival club and I asked the barman for another drink and he said no and I cried.'

CHAPTER 20

Giving support: you can only do your best

ike most dads, John likes nothing better than to come to the rescue and help his kids out of a pickle. Not long ago, we were about to tuck into some much-anticipated pancakes for breakfast when John's mobile rang. It was Jordie.

'Hi Pa, how's it going? Yeah, look, I'm sitting in my car and I think it's broken down. Yeah, it's not starting ... No, I don't think it would be petrol. Well, yeah, the gauge has been on empty but I thought ... Where am I? I'm right at the entrance to the freeway, just near CityLink ... in the middle lane and I'm on a steep kind of hill ...'

John was immediately up and running to the shed to get our jerry can. Then his mobile rang again. It was

Bonnie. She was due to start work at 9 am at the kidswear shop where she had a part-time job but she was deadlocked inside her boyfriend's first-floor flat; he'd gone to work and taken the keys. Could John come over with the extension ladder so that she could climb out the window?

Could he? These are the moments John lives for, and as I watched him head off to his trusty station wagon, a jerry can in one hand and an extension ladder in the other, the only item he seemed to be missing was a super hero's cape.

Of course, these days Jordie is a well-established and respected member of Melbourne's thriving independent music scene. Sadly for John, this means Jordie no longer needs him to be his roadie, lugger, sound-mixer, chauffeur and all-important 'merch' seller after the gigs. In fact, Jordie awkwardly admitted that having someone as old as John selling his CDs may have put people off buying it. On the other hand, the great and glorious news for John, news that really put a spring in his step, was Bonnie's announcement that she was now an 'installation' artist. Even better for John was that Bonnie was an installation artist who didn't drive − talk about an unending opportunity to be needed.

After passing her VCE, Bonnie was accepted into the Victorian College of the Arts, specifically the painting department where, in the three years she was there, she never once, not once, touched a brush or paints. Apparently painting was 'just so yesterday'.

College was where Bonnie first discovered her passion for creating 'installations', a passion, as it turned out, that her father shared. It has formed a bond between them that is so strong I'm almost jealous (but mostly I'm relieved as it means I don't have to be involved in any way, which means I don't have to do anything whatsoever to help, which means at the end of the day, I'm really happy because I can just kick back and drink my wine while they race around like maniacs). Together John and Bonnie head off in the Camry station wagon and, with all the adventurous spirit and excitement of an outback safari, they prowl suburban back streets, laneways and second-hand building suppliers looking for 'stuff'. They arrive back at number 26 and deepen their bond by stealthily sneaking all the 'stuff' down the side path and into the shed, all the while hoping I don't see them and start crying because 'all I've ever wanted is a place free from clutter!' John has taught Bonnie to hammer, saw and nail. He gave her a power-drill for her birthday. When one of Bonnie's outdoor installations – consisting of a lounge suite, coffee-table, fan, lamp and doorframe with a door hanging from it – almost blew away after an uncharacteristically wild storm (the media referred to it as a mini-hurricane), John showed nothing but sympathy and immediately headed off in the car with a distraught Bonnie and helped her put it back together. Two days later, this piece won a major award. John wept with pride.

Once, when Bonnie had a piece exhibited in a tiny shop-window in the Flinders Street subway, the bubble machine she was using went on the blink. When she expressed concern, a friend suggested, 'Don't worry, if worse comes to worst and the bubble machine stops working, your dad will probably lie in the window and blow the bubbles himself.'

And John would almost rather die than miss one of Bonnie's exhibition openings. For one such event, as part of a large group show that was held in an underground carpark, Bonnie created a miniature bedroom with four walls, a ceiling and a door. It stood about one metre tall and you had to crawl inside on your hands and knees, lie on a double mattress and gaze up at the ceiling, which was beautifully adorned with lights and featured images of Bonnie's boyfriend and the words, 'Are You Awake?'

The day before the opening, John had been running a circus workshop and was demonstrating the correct way to fall when wearing a pair of stilts. Unfortunately, from both a personal and professional perspective, John managed to tear both his quadriceps while following his own instructions. In fact, he managed to tear them so badly that he couldn't bend his legs at all and had to walk like a robot.

Despite being in excruciating pain, John refused to consider missing an event that was so important to his daughter. He winced in agony as he forced his legs to bend and painfully crawled inside Bonnie's 'bedroom'.

We lay on the mattress together 'experiencing' the work and it was indeed very impressive. I was so tired I could have happily dozed off except that there was a queue waiting outside to come in. I turned over onto all fours and proceeded to crawl out backwards. I waited for John to appear but he was a no show. I popped my head back inside the little bedroom. John looked terrible, his face twisted in pain. 'It's my legs,' he said. 'I can't move them. I can't get out.'

I crawled back inside to help him. He tried turning over on his stomach and shimmying backwards like a worm but it was no good. He turned over and lay on his back again, trying to wriggle his body forward; nothing doing. We discussed our options. We could call an ambulance or we could dismantle Bonnie's artwork from around him. We agreed that both solutions could possibly cause our daughter to have a complete breakdown so I went in search of Jordie. I found him in a tee-pee construction chatting with some young arty women who wore exotically short shorts, fishnet singlet-tops, large gypsy earrings, heavy, dark eye make-up, and hair teased into massive beehives. Jordie was decidedly unimpressed when I sat down cross-legged next to him and whispered, 'It's your father ...'

While I kept an eye out for Bonnie, Jordie grabbed John's feet and simply dragged him out; his head clunked on the concrete as he was pulled off the mattress. 'Sorry, Dad, was I a bit quick?' Once outside the installation,

John put his arms around both our shoulders and with a great heave we stood him upright.

Bonnie appeared not long after. 'Hey Dad, how'd you like my room?'

'Loved it, Bonnie, absolutely loved it; could've spent the whole night in there.'

Of course, John's boundless optimism and pride in his children can be a total embarrassment for them. His enthusiasm can at times be so extreme that we've had to create a code. Often, when we're at an exhibition opening of Bonnie's or watching Jordie at a gig, I've been forced to mutter, 'Bring it back, John.'

'Is it getting too big?'

'Yeah, it is.'

But no matter how hard John tries, he can never reduce the width of his smile. It literally goes from ear to ear.

John also likes to show support for our children's artistic friends, and that's where it can become torturously embarrassing for all concerned. At one art exhibition, Bonnie's friend Katya was lying in the foetal position in a dark room, curled up on a small circle of dirt and surrounded by tiny candles that flickered in the pale light. I was in another part of the gallery at the time, thoroughly enjoying the work of a Sri Lankan artist (let's just say there was some painting and frames involved) when Bonnie came running over to me, looking distraught.

'Oh my God, Mum, it's Dad. He's just standing next to Katya. He's got his eyes closed and he's smiling and …

oh my God, Mum … he's humming, really loudly. Can you please go and get him?'

I did as I was told. 'John, Bonnie wants you to get out of here.'

'But the acoustics, Scotty … they're fantastic, and this image,' he gestured towards Katya, who remained totally still and quiet throughout the ensuing family saga. 'What a beautiful, peaceful image.'

'Yes, John, but you're embarrassing your daughter.'

'Scotty, I'm not just humming, I'm actually singing "Swing Low Sweet Chariot". It's what came to me as I was standing here. All I'm doing is responding to the art.'

'Well, can't you do it without the singing?'

'For God's sake, you people are so uptight.'

I'll come clean and confess that there are times when I don't get contemporary art. The day Bonnie arrived home, her face radiant with triumph, and pulled a dead bird out of her bag, gushing, 'I found it in the gutter, isn't it amazing?' I just looked at her and replied, 'It's a dead bird.' The night I was cooking dinner and yelled, 'Has anyone seen the good roasting pan?' only to have Bonnie confess some minutes later that she'd used it as part of an installation. I simply slumped.

'But don't worry, Mum, I brought it home. It's in my room somewhere.'

'Yeah, well, that may be the case but I haven't got twenty years to do an archaeological dig in your bedroom to find it,' whereupon I headed out the front door to buy a new one.

But just as I'd dragged my own mother out of her comfort zone and into the world of contemporary stand-up comedy, so my daughter dragged me into her world of contemporary art. And just as my mother found my comedy challenging, I admit there have been times when Bonnie and her friends' art has left me gasping, and when I say gasping, I mean gasping.

It was in a small, windowless room at the Victorian College of the Arts that I saw Bonnie's first-ever solo exhibition. I wanted to be supportive; of course I did, she's my daughter. I stood intently gazing at the poster-size photo of Bonnie wearing nothing but a bra and pants. She was holding a gun and staring down the barrel of the camera lens, looking at me with an expression not too dissimilar to that of Myra Hindley, the famous English Moors murderer. I started to read the accompanying text Bonnie had written. I hoped she didn't hear me gulp. I read three words and immediately recalled how I had once expected Mum to accept me swearing on TV, and now here I was in a small cupboard and I wasn't coping at all. I decided it was best I stop reading and study the picture again. Bonnie was looking at me looking at her picture. 'Are you alright, Mum?'

'Yes, I'm fine, why do you ask?'

'Because you're using your Ventolin.' And I was. I hadn't even realised.

At one group exhibition, I walked into the gallery and there on a gigantic video screen was a short film entitled, *My Cunt Smoking*. And that's exactly what the footage showed in graphic, close-up detail. Holy Hannah, the artist was indeed smoking from that part of her body. Immediately, I checked the artist's name. It wasn't Bonnie. Oh thank Christ for that. This meant I could relax and be 'intrigued' rather than 'mortified'. Quite frankly, I was agog. I knew vaginas were capable of popping ping-pong balls across stages in Bangkok nightclubs but I hadn't realised they could smoke. How did the artist discover this? I recalled how, when I used to visit Lynda at the Peter MacCallum hospital, I would see a woman sitting out the front in her wheelchair, smoking through her tracheotomy. I wondered how she would react to the news that there was an alternative. Then I started wondering how I would react if I were this artist's mother. How could I be supportive? What would my mother have done in such circumstances? Certainly, in this particular situation she no doubt would have had her fourth heart attack and died on the spot.

On one of the rare occasions that my mother came to see me perform at an all-female comedy night, actress Nolene Brown was also on the bill. The only comment my mother made afterwards was, 'That Nolene Brown … isn't her hair superb?' This strategy is often used by mothers not wanting to tell their children what they really think – I call it 'the maternal art of deflection'.

I stood staring at the cigarette as it blew smoke from that most intimate part of the female anatomy and decided that if I were this artist's mum, I would say, 'Gee, I didn't know you smoked ...'

CHAPTER 21

In praise of doubt and the occasional bout of self-loathing

ecently my children implied that I was to blame for their low self-esteem issues. They seemed to be quite cranky about it. Well, I was cranky that they were cranky.

Okay, so you suffer a little low self-esteem sometimes, so what? Get a grip. Some people inherit conditions from their mothers like dystonia, where all your muscles twitch involuntarily and your body jack-knifes so suddenly that one minute you're upright and the next second, *kapow*, you're bent over double, your ankles twisted and your feet looking as though they're on back to front. How would your self-esteem be then? And there's nothing wrong with a bit of self-doubt either. It can simply be that you're experiencing a case of good old-fashioned humility. And I love humility, it's very attractive; well, a lot more attractive than having a head so big you can't fit through the double doors of a tram. And self-loathing has been getting a negative rap that it doesn't necessarily deserve. I, for one, have very fond memories of the days when we were free to run around the paddocks full of it. Nobody gave a toss. You could hate your own guts and no one took any notice; it was considered perfectly normal behaviour. We didn't have Oprah or Dr Phil crapping on about how to love yourself even though you're as fat and ugly and dumb as a huge steaming turd plopped fresh from a cow's arse. And I don't care if I'm accused of bad parenting. Let Human Services read this and come knocking on my door to take my children away from me. They're in their twenties now; it's time they moved out anyway.

I once read about a Tibetan village in which the villagers were so dirt-poor that in winter up to fifty family members plus their yaks (whose poo kept them warm) shared a single room. Apart from the concept of using poo instead of central gas heating to keep warm, what amazed me was that these people had no concept of low self-esteem. They were happy, joyful people who simply didn't understand what feeling lousy about yourself meant.

If I ever met one of these Tibetan villagers I'd cut straight to the chase: 'You don't know what low self-esteem is? Are you for real? What on earth do you talk about? I couldn't imagine a conversation in which I didn't mention being an overweight, unfit, borderline alcoholic with an embarrassing amount of facial hair and a disappointing career.'

'Ah, I see,' the happy Tibetan villager would reply, 'So this is low self-esteem?'

'Yes, I suppose it is.'

'Ah, so now I understand. Low self-esteem is what we in Tibet call truth.'

Now, I'm probably in the minority when I admit to being proud that Australia as a nation suffers tremendous low self-esteem. I think it's a refreshingly marvellous and unique characteristic. One of the greatest examples of our nation swimming in a sea of self-doubt took place in the year 2000. It was the lead-up to the Olympic Games in Sydney and it seemed that everywhere you turned – coffee-shops, public transport, supermarket queues, the TAB, laundromats, hairdressers, offices, corporate conferences, school yards, doctors' waiting rooms, hospital wards, women giving birth, talkback radio, current affairs programs – all of us, in one way or another, were asking the same question: 'What if our opening ceremony is shithouse?'

We were a population on the verge of suffering a massive, communal, mental breakdown. All classes, all creeds, all races were united in sharing a simmering, low-key but nevertheless painful anxiety attack. Not since the declaration of the Second World War had we shown such a united front – except in 1939 we believed we could be the winners. But when it came to our Olympics opening ceremony, an event that was going to be broadcast live to billions and billions of people all around the world, we weren't just swimming in self-doubt, we were drowning in it. And fair enough. I mean, let's face it, none of us had ever really recovered from the excruciating embarrassment of seeing the blow-up kangaroos riding two-wheeler bicycles at the handover ceremony in Atlanta four years earlier. Oh God, what would Australia do at the actual opening ceremony? I heard someone on the tram hypothesising, 'Do you think it'll be Rolf Harris singing "Jake the Peg"?' Oh Jesus wept, give us all a glass of spiked lime Kool-Aid and let's kill ourselves now.

Two days before the opening ceremony John was overcome with a sudden wave of patriotic fervour. We were sleeping in when suddenly at about 9.10 am he leapt out of bed, threw on some clothes and, like a man possessed, ran down the street to our corner shops where he marched into Hexter and Eddy's electrical store and purchased our first-ever new TV. It was a big wide-screen thing that was way too enormous to fit into our tiny lounge area, but who cares about such details when an event of such historic proportions was about to take place in OUR land? OUR home! OUR birthplace!

My dad Russ had done exactly the same thing forty-four years earlier in 1956 when the Games were held in Melbourne. He raced out and bought one of the first black and white TV sets and put it on our front porch. All the neighbours brought their own chairs and sat on our front lawn cheering on Betty Cuthbert to yet another gold medal. People were more relaxed then because back in those days everyone was happy with an opening ceremony in which a local marching band did a lap of the oval, the scouts and girl-guide troupes did some semaphore work and the Queen of England made a speech. What could go wrong, apart from a wayward semaphore flag flying into the crowd and taking someone's eye out, which, according to my research, never happened?

But in 2000, so much could go hideously wrong. On the day of the historic event our friends gathered at number 26 to watch it unravel on the new TV. The barbie was sizzling with marinated chicken and gourmet sausages. There were big platters of coleslaw and potato salad. There was lots of champagne, beer, wine and soft drinks but I couldn't eat. I was too nervous. It goes without saying that I could still drink.

The ceremony started; you could feel the entire nation tensing, preparing to be part of the biggest embarrassment in the history of world entertainment. But what the hell? Within minutes our hearts were soaring and tears were flowing as we witnessed a brilliant, unbelievably beautiful, artistic event that featured powerful Australian images and an evocative, emotional story. As long as I live I will never forget that first glimpse of something in the distant sky sweeping towards Homebush Stadium. I was trying to listen to the TV commentary but all my friends were talking.

'Look!'

'What?'

'Where?'

'There, in the sky.'

'Where?'

'Here.'

'Don't stand in front of the telly, Liz.'

'I'm just pointing out this thing.'

'What thing?'

'Look, here, see in the corner of the screen? That thing in the sky.'

'What is it?'

'Is it a bird?'

'Is it a plane?'

'No, it's Nicki Webster.'

Of course, we didn't know her name until the following morning when she appeared on the front page of newspapers all around the world. All we knew was that as a nation we gasped in wonder when we realised that this tiny 'thing' in the sky was a small white child with blonde curls, a big bow in her hair and a polka-dot dress who appeared to be gracefully cartwheeling towards the earth in slow motion. We held our collective breath as we then saw her being gently caught in the welcoming and reassuring arms of an Aboriginal elder wearing traditional tribal paint. John was bawling his eyes out, making spluttery, choking noises as he does when he watches something emotionally moving on the TV. Sure, we Australians have our problems, but right then and there, we could all stand tall and stand proud. As our friend Liz said through her tears when a singing Kylie Minogue appeared on top of a giant thong, 'What a fucking great show. Doesn't it make you proud?' Proud! We were so proud. What a magnificent land we come from. What a great people we are! What a nation! What a show!

Imagine if Australians had believed from the get-go that it was going to be great: where's the fun in that? Where's the journey from wracking, crippling doubt to overwhelming, soaring triumph?

A few days after my children expressed their disappointment about inheriting the low self-esteem gene, I was reading my horoscope in the *Herald Sun*. I must stress, this is truly what Jonathan Cainer had in store for Taureans that day: 'Have you ever considered that your self-doubt is simply a way of coping with your extraordinary genius, and the reason you constantly talk yourself down is because you don't want others to always feel overshadowed by you?'

I couldn't believe it. What fantastic news! But as I read further, I realised to my dismay that Mr Cainer was being sarcastic in both tone and sentiment. So I got the scissors and cut out only those first, positive sentences. I swaggered into the kitchen where Jordie and Bonnie were having a snack. 'Here's something you might be interested in reading ...'

CHAPTER 22

We all do it

can't believe that when I first moved into number 26 I hated it so much that I wept inconsolably and didn't have a good thing to say about it. This was cruel, insensitive and naive of me because in twenty-three years this house has never let me down, not once. When all else has not been great, it's always been here, somehow providing a stable base and a haven from the stresses and strains of the outside world. And it never stops coming up trumps.

Recently we urgently had to find hostel accommodation for my mum. Where was the one place that could miraculously take her in that very day? A place that was walking distance from number 26, that's where. For a daughter who doesn't drive and feels extreme guilt about her mother, and for that matter extreme love, this single event made buying this house all those years ago worth it.

To be brutally honest, the only reason I've been able to write this book is because Mum has Alzheimer's and let's just say her priorities have changed. For a start, there's all the swearing. Mum would never have coped even though I've recently been reading Stephen King's book *On Writing*, in which he suggests that yes, swearing in literature is lazy but if that's how a person talks, what can you do? Right on, brother, you've got to be truthful. (But then again, my mum isn't Stephen King.)

In another writing tip he suggests that I (yes, I do believe that Stephen King was talking directly, in fact *only*, to me, such is the loneliness and madness experienced by a vulnerable first-time author) finish my first draft as quickly as possible so that self-doubt can't catch up and overtake me. Oh dear, I've always been such a fan of self-doubt but now I was an even bigger fan of Stephen's writing advice so I took off and ran like the blazes until ...

... I had to stop. Mum's unwanted companion, Alzheimer's, was beginning to really wreak havoc.

I was working on breakfast radio at the time. This meant getting up at 4.15 every morning, arriving at work to read the papers and plan the show at 5 am, going on air at 6 am and then being upbeat, witty, funny, knowledgeable, controversial and compelling for the next three hours. (This was the brief, not necessarily the reality and, for what it's worth, these days whenever I hear the word 'compelling', I audibly groan, feel an overwhelming sense of hopelessness and want to throw up.) The three hours on air would be followed by meetings and planning sessions, then home for a sleep, and in the afternoon you were expected to live your life in such a way that anything — and I mean anything — could be converted into a story for the following morning's show. Such events ranged from the weather — 'How did you keep cool yesterday? Give us a call.' — to the price of zucchinis — 'Why are zucchinis so expensive at the moment? How much have you paid for them? What do you do with your zucchinis? Give us a call.' — to personal stories — 'John woke me up in the middle of the night with the loudest fart. What does your partner do that drives you crazy? Give us a call.' In the evenings you'd watch news and current affairs programs and then popular shows such as *Big Brother*, *Australian Idol* or *Dancing with the Stars*. Then at about 9.30 you would begin to feel slightly sick as a quiet panic set in about getting to bed so that you had enough time to sleep before you had to get up again.

It was during this period of my life that my mum's Alzheimer's began to take a much firmer grip. She was living at home on her own, the same humble war-service house she'd been in for the past fifty years. Since she'd spent most of her working life nursing at the geriatric hospital across the road she had a particularly strong dread of going into a nursing home and made my sister and me kind of, sort of promise that we would never put her in one.

But for the final six months that Mum was living at home there was not a waking moment that I wasn't worried about her. My sister Julie was the same. We both suffered terrible insomnia and headaches. We were waiting for the 'disaster'. According to what we'd been told, the 'disaster' would be the clincher that would mean Mum would have to go into care. The 'disaster' could be anything – from getting lost to getting sick from not eating to no longer recognising us.

As it was, Mum no longer remembered to eat, and cooking was too confusing. Sometimes she didn't recall how to turn her beloved radio on and she no longer watched television. She couldn't remember appointments and she became paranoid that people, including her children and grandchildren, were stealing from her. The customer service person at Mum's local bank would ring and tell me she was worried about Mum heading off and walking home alone through the park. 'She just seems so vulnerable.' Mum actually set a record at the bank as the first person to lose her passbook so often (she never had a key-card) that she went into double figures; she had twelve passbooks in two years. In the end they kept it at the bank for her. Then there was the next-door neighbour who rang to explain that he'd removed Mum's back door because she was locked out, having lost yet another key. Her neighbour on the other side rang to tell me that he'd climbed into Mum's roof because she was sure she could hear noises. The district nurse rang to say he'd caught

Mum, at eighty years of age, climbing in through her kitchen window because once more she'd lost her key. The daycare worker rang to say, 'Don't panic but your Mum is missing. She wasn't at home when I called in to give her lunch. I've been to all her usual haunts, Kentucky Fried, the bank, the park; she's nowhere to be seen.' Eventually Mum would turn up, explaining that she 'had probably been out with someone else, but honestly I can't remember who the blazes it was, or where we went'. Then there was the woman from a community services office at the local shopping centre who rang to say that she had Mum there with her but Mum didn't know where she was or how to get home. There are very good people in this world and Mum was lucky to be surrounded by some of them.

And of course there were Mum's own phone calls.

'Hello Denise.'

'Mum, how are you?'

'Well, I'm in a terrible state.'

'What's happened?'

'Well, it seems I have no money.'

'Mum, why do you say that?'

'Well, I just haven't.'

'Mum, you have got quite a lot of money.'

'Have I?'

'Yes, it's in the bank. Julie and I are looking after it for you. You've got a lot of savings, Mum, don't worry.'

'Are you sure?'

'Mum, I'm positive.'

'Oh well, that's great news. Oh, that's the best news I've heard in a long time.'

Five minutes later the phone would ring again.

'Hello Denise.'

'Mum, what's wrong?'

'Well, I don't seem to have any money ...'

The district nurse would come once a day, and a carer would come for an hour or so each weekday. John and I went to Mum's every Saturday and Sunday to cook and eat with her. My sister, who lived some distance away, would visit once a week. But there are twenty-four hours in a day and often Mum spent twenty-three of them on her own. This, combined with my breakfast radio routine, meant that I spent most of my waking, and for that matter my sleeping, hours with my nerve-ends sticking out of my skin. Often I was quite literally deranged with tiredness and stress.

Twice I exploded at work as I've never exploded before. Actually, I lost my mind. As I explained to the two people on the receiving end of my outrage: my colleague, comedian Shaun Micallef, and my radio producer, Annie Winton, 'Well, if it's any comfort, you've joined a very exclusive club. The only other person I've ever abused like that is John, so in a way it makes my relationship with you pretty special.'

Then came the phone call from the ambulance officers. Mum had called an ambulance but by the time it arrived she'd forgotten her problem. As it turned out, there was indeed a medical problem, which consequently turned out to be the promised 'disaster'.

This is the point in time when you put your hands in the air and say, 'This is it. My mum can't be on her own for one more minute.' This is as much as you know. You do not know what you will do next but whatever it is, you suspect it's going to be cataclysmic. My sister and I both declared that we would leave work if that's what it took to get Mum cared for. And we would've, because when it comes to the crunch and a loved one desperately needs your help, you surprise yourself with your response. But neither my sister nor I had to leave work. (Oh my God, was I relieved.) In our panicked, desperate state, we found Mum some respite care close to number 26.

The morning Mum was to go into the hostel, she was extraordinary. John and I had stayed the night with her, sleeping in the Queen Anne single beds. I'd been awake throughout the night with a thumping headache and vomiting with the enormity of what was to take place the following day. Mum knew something momentous and terrifying was happening and there she was, first thing in the morning, standing in her kitchen. The radio was on. The table was set with cloth, plates, cups and saucers, jams, butter, milk and sugar. She had made a pot of tea and there was a stack of hot, crisp toast awaiting us. She knew that this was her last-ditch attempt to prove that she was fine.

John and I appeared in the kitchen. Mum looked shocked. 'Where's Beb and Ron?'

'Pardon, Mum?'

'Where's Beb and Ron?'

'I guess they're in Perth, where they live.'

'Oh, I thought they were here.'

'No, Mum.'

'So was that you and John who were sleeping in that bedroom?'

'Yes, Mum, it was.'

'Oh, I don't know where I got the idea that it was Beb and Ron.'

'Look, Mum, I know you're disappointed but do we still get the breakfast?'

Beb and Ron, Mum's brother and sister-in-law, had stayed with Mum some twenty years earlier.

Julie arrived and we had to tell Mum that she was going into respite. She's no fool; she knew what 'respite' could mean. She busied herself cleaning up the house. I packed her small vinyl suitcase, finding a new toilet-bag, which had a new toothbrush, toothpaste and a cake of soap in a container that she'd obviously had ready in case of an emergency. For fifty years Mum had lived in her home and here we were on this seemingly normal day packing her bag, all of us knowing deep down that she would never set foot inside it again.

It was time to go. Mum said, 'Hang on, there's something I've got to do.' She went and ironed a hanky which she put in her handbag. She straightened the towels in her bathroom and folded the face-washer and put it neatly beside the basin.

Julie and I were seated in the hostel manager's office. We'd been greeted at the locked doors of the dementia unit by a happy, black, curly-haired dog and an enormously fat cat. The manager explained that this respite bed was in fact a permanent place, if we decided that's what we wanted. Without hesitating, Julie and I said, 'We want it.' It was then explained that the accommodation bond would cost $200,000.

'Oh,' I said, trying to sound casual, 'and how do we get that sort of money?'

'Does your mother own a house?'

'Yes.'

'Well, you sell it.'

Oh Jesus. Between us, my sister and I had never sold a house before, let alone sold our mother's treasured haven without telling her to put her into accommodation she had always openly derided. If ever Stephen King's advice to just dive in and do something as quickly as possible before self-doubt overtakes was applicable, it was now – and I hadn't even read his book then.

My sister and I packed up Mum's house with little time for reflection or emotion. It sold quickly. We took Mum's photos to put in her room at the hostel. We hung her tapestries, which she'd spent so many hours making, up on her wall. Her two floral lounge chairs we placed near her bed. And her crocheted rug we put on her bed.

As a child, having spent a good deal of time hanging out at the nursing home where Mum worked, I grew to hate them. I hated the smell and I hated the uselessness of an existence spent lying in bed doing nothing until relief arrived in the form of death.

I was amazed to visit Mum at the hostel one day to be invited to join her in a yoga class, and then to learn about the weekly singalongs and the painting classes. There are great residents, such as the woman who always wears two different shoes, the woman who tells you that she loves you and how beautiful you are, and the smokers who hang out in the courtyard with an air of 'cool' about them. It was amazing to see my mum swing into her old nursing days mode, helping others to go to the toilet (even when they didn't want to, but she insisted). She helps feed other residents, gives them reassuring cuddles, and tells me what I have to do to assist the other patients.

Visiting the dementia unit is like therapy for me. Often I arrive there to have Joan, one of the residents, ask, 'How old are you?'

'Fifty-three.'

'Such a baby. I wish I was as young as you.'

During the federal elections, another resident, Jean, was very up with the current political news. She was a huge fan of Maxine McKew. 'Have you ever thought of getting into politics?' she asked me.

'No, no, I haven't, Jean.'

'Well, you should. I think you would make an excellent prime minister of Australia. What do you think?' Jean asked a nearby group of residents, 'Don't you think she would make an excellent prime minister?' They all agreed that I would.

Wow. So what if it's a dementia unit? A compliment's a compliment.

The first time I took our dog Raffi to the hostel, he was so overcome that he did a big poo in the middle of the dining room/sitting room area. I didn't have a bag on me and I couldn't attract a member of staff so I desperately tried to stop elderly people from walking on it. One resident, who at that stage of her Alzheimer's could only speak French, was heading straight for it. 'Non, non, Leonie, non! Ne marche pas, um … um … merde, Leonie, *merde*.' I was doing my best with my limited recall of schoolgirl French.

Leonie looked at me as if to say, 'You're standing astride a piece of poo, speaking in weird French, and *I'm* the one in a dementia unit?'

I leant down and apologised to an old lady sitting nearby. She looked at me incredulously. 'Why are you apologising, darling?'

'Well, because my dog has just done a big poo at your feet, Teresa.'

She was adamant. 'You must never apologise for something like that; after all darling, we all do it, don't we?'

'Sure, I agree with you Teresa, we all do poo, but not in the middle of a public dining room.'

She leant towards me conspiratorially, 'Actually, darling, I think most of us in here have done exactly that.' And we laughed our heads off.

These days Mum and I often sit outside in the small courtyard. Mum loves to see the sky; she always marvels at its beauty. 'Look at that blue sky. Have you ever seen anything like it? I'm sure the sky is getting bluer and bluer.' Minutes will pass as we continue to gaze upward and then Mum will say something like, 'And what have you been up to lately?'

And I will reply, 'Oh, not much, still plodding on with my book. I don't know why but it's taking me forever.'

'Is there some reason that you have to hurry?'

'No, not really.'

'Well, take your time then. I imagine writing a book is something that can't be rushed. What's it about?'

'Oh, well, Mum, it's about family. You're in it.'

'Oh dear.'

'But don't worry, Mum, you can always sue.'

When I leave the hostel, I always say, 'Come with me and we'll say goodbye at the border, Mum.' And she accompanies me as far as the large glass double doors. She cups my face and her blue eyes sparkle with love, pride and appreciation. She kisses me and says, 'Thanks a million for coming.' I always sincerely answer, 'It's a pleasure.' I key in the code and the double doors slide open. I step through to the other side. Mum has never attempted to come with me. As I walk away, I turn and see Mum, still watching me, so tiny and vulnerable. She waves. I wave back and Raffi and I head home to number 26.

CHAPTER 23
As things currently stand

I am scared. I've been losing sleep. I'm about to head into murky territory, namely the present. It's terrifying.

Don't get me wrong; it's not as if we've got a body buried in the cellar – we don't have a cellar. It's just that my kids are adults now, which means I can't really talk about them anymore – at least that's what their lawyers have told me. I've been so stressed I sought advice from a book called *A Guide for the Advanced Soul*, a collection of inspirational quotes edited by Susan Hayward. On the cover, Susan promises that if I hold a problem in my mind, then open the book at any page, the answer will be there.

So I did as Susan instructed. I held the book. I closed my eyes. I asked the question, 'How do I write about the present?' I opened it up ...

> **Your subconscious mind has the solution and is
> waiting to reveal it to you. If an answer does not
> come, turn the problem over to your deeper mind,
> prior to sleep. Keep on turning your request over
> to your subconscious until the answer comes.**
> Brian Adams, 'How to Succeed'

Mmm. I would have preferred something a little more
concrete but beggars can't be choosers. That night I went
to bed and attempted to connect with my subconscious
mind.

The following morning I received my answer: 'Darl,
you've just got to fuckin' tell it how it is.'

Except this wasn't my subconscious speaking, it was
my friend Sal who quite by chance rang me that very
morning ... or was it chance? Whatever it was, it was
sound advice, so here are the facts.

There are still the five of us living at number 26. John
and I are in our fifties – make that *early* fifties. Jordie and
Bonnie are in their twenties – make that *early* twenties.

Raffi is eight – make that *fifty-six* in dog years.

John is the only one with a normal job. He is a director
of theatre festivals in schools that aim to promote the mental
health and wellbeing of children. He goes to an office and
gets paid a regular wage. He gets annual holidays,
superannuation, and he does something weird called salary
sacrificing, or something like that. Being a freelance artist, I
haven't the slightest interest in such details.

Bonnie is twenty-two and works mostly from home as a visual artist. She supports herself by working part-time at a childcare centre, borrowing from her parents and living frugally. She does all her clothes shopping on eBay. Recently she bought a pair of black leather boots for only $4 – pity they didn't fit her. Then there were the walking boots for which she paid $5. She wore them to work the next day and apparently they were really comfortable until both soles came off. She fixed them with gaffer tape – ah, how history does indeed repeat itself.

Bonnie came close to moving out recently but at the last moment had an epiphany of sorts: 'Mum, why would I leave a comfortable home to go and rent some rat-infested hovel and live on two-minute noodles?' Had I been asked that same question at a similar age, my answer would have been 'Sex!' There was no way I could ever have indulged in this activity while living with Marg and Russ in Greensborough. The thought of making love to some young chap in my Queen Anne single bed while my sister pretended to be asleep in the bed opposite and my glow-in-the-dark Jesus stared down at me from his cross had no appeal whatsoever.

Don't get me wrong. I don't wish to imply that simply because we bought Bonnie a comfy double bed when she was sixteen that she immediately started living like a loose hussy with no morals. Far from it. The fact is, she's been in a long-term relationship with the most delightful and, it has to be said, handsome young chap who John and I love. But even more to the point, Bonnie's bed appears to have become a storage area for her clothes, handbags, toiletries and art supplies. That she fits in there to sleep is a damn miracle.

Jordie is also still living at home. He requested, in fact he begged me, not to include this detail in the book – apparently it doesn't fit with his self-image of a struggling, drug- and alcohol-fuelled, fucked-up genius musician. 'Mum, please, I don't want people to know that I still live with you and Dad; it's humiliating.'

'Yeah, well, move out then,' was my sympathetic response.

Once again, out of respect for my family's privacy (then again, why start worrying at this stage?) I don't want to give away too many intimate details but I will state that I have had the pleasure of meeting the most exquisitely beautiful young women I've ever seen in my life because of Jordie, and sometimes they've only been wearing a towel. Now I'm making him sound like Hugh Hefner in the Playboy mansion but, as I often try to explain to my kids, my job is to make a story entertaining and sometimes this requires exaggeration. Exactly how much I'm exaggerating I'm not prepared to say but a beautiful young woman wearing a towel did once pass me on her way from our bathroom and beamed rapturously, 'Oh, hi there. You must be Jordie's mother.'

'No, I'm just part of the harem,' I replied, and then, after an awkward silence, I had to explain, 'I'm just joking.'

Jordie is about to make his first studio album with professional producers and paid musicians. He has to borrow most of the money from us as well as use the cash he's managed to save by continuing to live at home. He makes his income from gigs and selling his previous records, which were all made in our shed, his last one costing him a slab of beer for the musos.

Three years ago, John, Jordie and a builder from up the street called Dave converted the ugly, once-upon-a-time garage-then-shed into a recording studio. (No shenanigans during this renovation, I promise. Apart from anything else, these days I'd rather die than let a stranger see me in the nude.) The front aluminium wall was ripped off and replaced with weatherboards and a second-hand bay window featuring leadlight glass. Any music person will at this point be thinking: bay window in a recording studio? Dumb idea. But this is where John's ingenious invention of soundproof panels specifically designed to fit a bay window came into play.

Unfortunately, they didn't work. We discovered this when our new neighbours complained about the 'intolerable noise levels'. I was heartbroken. I knew it was a sign of the times a-changin'. For twenty years we'd lived in perfect harmony with our elderly Greek and Italian neighbours. We could have screaming arguments, noisy backyard cricket matches, adolescent gatherings, amplified bands, boozy parties, family gatherings – and so could our neighbours. There was an understanding that noise meant that life was being celebrated. But then this young, upwardly mobile, Anglo couple moved in and suddenly we had to worry about their bed-time. What? Apparently they had to get to sleep because they had to get up and go to work in the morning or some such nonsense. Talk about a couple of mood-sucking, *joie de vivre* killers! Being the mature adult in this situation, I advised Jordie, 'Oh, stuff them, they're just a pain in the arse. Keep making your music, son, and crank up the volume.'

But then the police started visiting ... regularly. Eventually the emotional stress got to Jordie. 'Ma, telling a muso they have to play music with their amp turned right down is like telling a hurdler to hurdle without legs – it's fucked.' Fair enough. And so the non-soundproof soundproof panels were ripped down from the windows, allowing the sunlight to pour in and the garage/shed/ recording studio became an artist's studio where Bonnie could construct her installations. Except that pretty soon Bonnie found she could no longer fit inside because her art installations took up all the available space so now it's officially back to being just a shed full of stuff – such is the cycle of life for a garage that you can't drive a car into.

It seems that these days kids tend to stay at home, living with their parents until they're about fifty-seven or fifty-eight years old. There are many reasons for this – economics being the major one. I'm happy, in fact it makes me feel good, to give my kids a good feed and a bit of financial and emotional support – that's what parents are for. And just in case it isn't obvious, I adore my kids and I could not be prouder of them.

But living with them is kind of doing my head in. It's not that they aren't great company – they are. It's not that they're difficult people – they're not. It's not that they don't bring a youthful vibrancy and excitement to the house – they do. It's the housework! It drives me nuts. In fact, it drives me from the house. Oh yes, on more than one occasion I've stormed out the front door late at night, John running after me looking worried.

'Scotty, where are you going?'

'I'm going to get a flat on my own and as far as I'm concerned you can all just stay here and drown in your own stinking mess.'

Then I would run to the nearby park and sit under a palm tree and quietly sob to myself that I was tired. Just tired. Tired of giving and getting fuck-all back.

(I used this line in a Comedy Festival show and was amazed that every single night all the middle-aged women in the audience burst into spontaneous applause.)

One positive to come out of such outbursts was that without fail, after about an hour sitting in the park, John would come and walk me home and I'd arrive to find the house in ship-shape form.

In more recent times I've let my housework standards drop. I do less, a lot less, but interestingly, nobody else does more to compensate. At one stage I tried writing notes and leaving them blue-tacked to walls all over the house. For instance, I penned the following to go above the kitchen bench: *As there are now four adults living in this house, think of it as a communal living situation. Thus, if you use the bench, please clear it after use. Love Mum.*

Above the dishwasher was this thought-provoking piece: *Don't leave dishes, rubbish or takeaway containers etc. on the sink. If you don't deal with them, who will? Love Mum.*

And just in case there was any confusion, I popped this suggestion on the dishwasher door: *If you go to put a dish in the dishwasher and find that it is FULL of CLEAN dishes, then UNSTACK it and put the dishes away! Love Mum.*

The notes didn't work.

To be fair, my kids do cook and they do their own washing. The fact that Jordie tends to whip up a meal of marinated lamb kebabs and a salad at 4 am is not a problem. However, putting on a load of washing at this hour has been cause for confrontation. I don't understand the scientific reason but the location of our laundry in relation to our bedroom means that when the machine reaches its final spin-cycle, our bedroom shakes so violently and the accompanying noise is so loud that John and I wake in fright thinking we're careening down a runway in a jumbo jet piloted by a drunken eighteen-year-old.

There is another drawback to living with my adult kids – the fact that we are all 'artists' working from home. This means that our house is always 'on'. There is no rest period. There is always someone awake trying to finish a project or at least worrying about how they will ever finish it when there is still 'so much to do'. There is no routine and no structure. Usually an evening meal is planned but no one is ever sure who will cook it (usually John), when it will be ready (any time between 7 and 10 pm) and who will be there to eat it (usually just John and me).

Even Raffi gets stressed wondering if anyone will manage to break out of their self-absorbed state long enough to take him for a walk. (Usually I do, but only after Raffi has sat at my feet while I'm at the computer and barked continuously for forty-five minutes.)

Creating original work in whatever field brings the artist enormous satisfaction and fulfilment but it can also bring crippling bouts of self-doubt. These days number 26 is no longer a haven, it is a pulsating hub of neuroses ranging from constant low-level anxiety to complete meltdowns resulting in tears of frustration at one's own inadequacies. (This latter display is limited to the female members of the house while the males attempt to reassure us that it's probably just our hormones.)

I know, I know. I have only recently been carrying on about the wonders of self-doubt but life moves forward and can bring unexpected changes, and the truth is I've done a backflip (hey, I'm only human). I am now having serious doubts about my belief in self-doubt. As a mother, you are naturally inclined to absorb your kids' anxieties.

You want to help carry their burden because you hate to see them suffer. This response kicks in as soon as you give birth – all you want to do is take that crying little baby in your arms and love and protect and feed it, even though you might have other things on your mind, like a torn vagina, for instance. This instinct doesn't change just because your kids become adults, which is why it's good if they move out – you don't see them much and so you are blissfully ignorant of their day-to-day mini-dramas.

But because I do live with my kids and because we are all artists and because we all work from home and because I am their mother, I am now carrying a triple load of self-doubt and quite frankly that's just too much for one human being to bear. Of course, I'm well aware that 'problems' in life are all relative. If I met a Chinese woman and she started to tell me about losing her home and all her family members in the Sichuan earthquake, I wouldn't interrupt her with, 'Oh, tell me about it, I've had a shocker of a week myself ... all the self-doubt I've been experiencing lately, it's been a nightmare.'

I guess I'm just trying to tell it how it is. Put it this way, I recently went out to dinner with John and his work colleagues who, like John, all work in the area of mental health. When I sincerely explained that John was the 'sane, rational, calm' member of our house, they looked utterly horrified. As my friend Sal said, 'Jeez, you know you've really got a fuckin' problem when John's the sanest member of your house.'

I know this is just another phase of life and that things will change. John and I have talked about what we'll do when the kids do move out. I rather fancy turning one of their bedrooms into a yoga retreat; John would quite like a music room. Then again, John also wants to buy the house next door, which sits on an enormous block of land, and build enviro-friendly mudbrick-style units and set up an old-age hippie commune. Yeah, we still have dreams and hopes, that's for sure.

Whatever the future, it seems that for now at least, John and I will be staying at number 26.

THE ALLERGY-FREE GUM ARABIC RUBBER BIRTHDAY CAKE

(wheat-free, egg-free, dairy-free, sugar-free, nut-free, taste-free)

> ½ cup dairy free margarine
> 3 tbsp pure maple syrup
> 1 tsp cinnamon
> 1 tsp nutmeg
> 1 tsp mixed spice
> 1½ cups rice flour
> 1½ cups barley flour
> 1 tsp baking soda
> pinch of salt
> 2 tsp baking powder
> 1½ cups water
> 1 tsp vanilla essence
> 1½ cups mashed pumpkin
> 125 ml coconut cream

Preheat oven to 190 degrees. Cream margarine and add maple syrup. Set aside.

Sift together cinnamon, nutmeg, mixed spice, flour, baking soda and salt, and set aside. Dissolve baking powder in ¼ cup water, then add to the margarine mixture.

Mix remaining water with vanilla, and add the pumpkin. Stir well. Add to margarine mixture. Combine the dry ingredients and the wet ingredients. Blend well. Taste-test mixture. (Note: don't be fooled by its gobsmacking blandness. You MUST allow at least 15–30 seconds for the extraordinarily bitter aftertaste to kick in.)

At this stage you will need to add more maple syrup. Keep adding until there is no more left and then scream at your partner to quickly go and get at least six more bottles.

When your mixture finally tastes sweet enough, you will most likely find that it's now too 'wet'. Allow yourself a minute to slump in despair, then picture your child's raw little face. Hold on to this image and begin to re-thicken the cake mix by frantically throwing in any allergy-free ingredients you can find in the cupboard – soy flour, rice flour, agar agar, leftover adzuki bean pilau.

By now your mixture will be so big, it will more than likely no longer fit in the mixing bowl. Try not to panic but timing at this point is crucial so for God's sake hurry! Find a bigger container! Don't be fussy. Just grab something. Anything. Yes, by all means grab the bucket you used yesterday to mop your putrid floors – the cooking process will kill the germs.

Pour the mixture into a cake tin and bake for 1 hour. (Note: Do not wait for it to rise; it won't.)

Bonus cooking tip: While cake is baking, drink a bottle of wine or whatever alcoholic beverage you can get your hands on.

Carefully remove from oven and cool. Cover cake in icing made from coconut cream and a little water, mixed together until a dull grey colour, and saw into slabs.

Serving suggestion: Don't.

Acknowledgements

First and foremost, a big thank you to Fran Berry at Hardie Grant for being adventurous enough to suggest I may have a book in me and, when I looked at her as though she was simply crazed and delusional, proceeded to offer to publish whatever that book might turn out to be.

And as for Emma Schwarcz, also from Hardie Grant, what can I say? 'Thanks' just doesn't convey how much I appreciate the hours this young woman, who has her whole life before her, spent wading through my first draft. Not only was her feedback insightful and constructive but it was so tactfully presented that I didn't even feel like killing myself. Not once did Emma say: 'Denise, this stinks.' Instead she said: 'Denise, perhaps you need a little more focus.' What a woman! In fact, (and this could be because I've spent so many years working in the crusty, cranky, hard-bitten world of comedy) I found everyone at Hardie Grant so darn nice and supportive and positive and, dare I say, happy that at times I've almost swooned and found myself a bit weepy with gratitude (then again, that could be menopause).

Then there's Nadine Davidoff with whom I developed an intense clandestine online affair, which I believe in modern literature is referred to as the editing process. All I can say is Nadine, I've never met you but I know without a doubt that I love you and I thank god you exist.

As for Judith Lucy, as always she's been a wonderful and supportive friend, offering to read my manuscript and provide a quote for the cover, and she didn't even charge me ... much.

Thanks to the entire team at Token, especially Dioni Meliss and Kevin Whyte, for your hard work, support and encouragement. I love being managed by you guys!

To all family and friends who appear in the book – sorry. (If it's any consolation I thank you. It's because of all of you and the richness you bring to my life that I have any stories to tell.) To all family and friends who don't appear in the book – sorry. (But don't worry, your turn will come. I don't know when, I don't know where but trust me, it will come.)

Finally I want to acknowledge the gutsiness and generosity of my kids, Jordie and Bonnie. I thank them from the bottom of my heart for allowing me to tell our story through my eyes ... although, come to think of it, they never really had much of a choice. Anyway, Bonnie said before she read the book, 'Mum, I'm assuming I'll feel embarrassed rather than hurt?' I replied that I thought that would be the case. She said, 'Then that's fine. Embarrassment I can deal with, it's hurt I can't handle.' (Oh god ... fingers crossed.)

Last of all, John. What an extraordinary man! Not only did he have to accept the fact that I was writing a book about our intimate life together but he had to then read every word I wrote and he had to do so while I sat and watched him intently, saying things like, 'What's wrong? You look unhappy. Don't you like it? Do you think it's funny? You do? But how come your brow is furrowed?' I offer my thanks and eternal love to this man, who once described life with me as 'a magnificent struggle'. Ditto, John, ditto.